Raised Bed Gardening

The Backyard Gardening Guide to an Organic Vegetable Garden and the Best Way to Grow Herbs, Fruit Trees, and Flowers in Raised Beds

Contents

Introduction

Raised bed gardening isn't a new method of growing plants; people have been reaping the benefits for centuries. One of the earliest recorded references about this method of gardening was in Liber de Cultura Hortorum by Walahfrid Strabo, a German Benedictine who praised gardens with poems written in Latin hexameters, also called the little garden or hortulus.

Although it is an ancient horticultural concept, raised bed gardening has suddenly become popular again, especially in overpopulated urban regions with limited gardening space. It is the perfect solution if you want to cultivate your own food or simply own a decorative garden. They are flexible and can be constructed in and for tiny spaces, including paved and concrete areas. If the current garden has no soil, it can be supplemented with any soil of preference.

This book is a comprehensive guide with easy-to-follow chapters. It begins with the basics, which will take you through the concept of raised bed gardening, the advantages of engaging in the practice, and everything you need to know before getting started. Reading further, you will be educated on the materials and tools of the trade, especially the materials from which you can construct your raised beds.

It also advises on the preparation and construction of your garden, including positioning to maximize sunlight, which is especially important, as you will discover soon enough. If the garden will be constructed in frost pockets or shade, this book is your go-to guide for suitable plant suggestions. You will also be provided with tips to help you design your garden layout to create textural and thrilling color combos. As you read further, you will discover various ways to identify and handle common plant diseases and pests.

After internalizing the basics, we'll look at the different raised bed gardens you can construct, including everything from purchasing already constructed products to making your own bed from scratch with the use of recycled materials.

You'll also learn about the less popular raised bed garden options such as the keyhole garden bed, which is an example of a sustainable raised bed that is mostly found in Africa. It features a universal compost heap and is built from any free materials that surround the area, like rocks excavated from poor soil. Another type of less popular raised bed is the hügelkultur, which originates from Northern Europe. It involves constructing beds over rotting tree stumps and timber, which slowly decompose to produce nutrients and improve the soil. One of the most attractive features of raised bed gardening is that everything from proper construction to actual planting can be done by yourself.

This book is rich in suggestions for what you can create or build from the comfort of your own home and in the privacy of your own space. You will discover a variety of planting schemes to choose from according to your personal circumstances and preferences. These varieties range from mini orchards to vegetable plots and even Japanese gardens. There are also options for people without an actual garden, like green roof space and window boxes.

I hope you will be inspired by this book to delve into the world of cultivating plants in raised beds. Whether you own a little courtyard, a grand walled garden, or a community garden, this method of gardening will improve and enhance your outdoor space organically and aesthetically. Once you get started, the ease of gardening will ensure that you never look back.

Chapter One: What is Raised Bed Gardening?

Gardening can be difficult to do, especially if you're struggling with a physical disability, you have issues with mobility, or you simply choose to enjoy your later years in life without having aches and pains in your legs and back. Constantly bending forward can make gardening difficult for some people, and this is where raised beds come into the picture, with a host of other advantages.

Definition

Raised bed gardening is a method of farming that provides areas for cultivation on rocky ground and raises the garden to a level that is more comfortable for the gardener. This method of gardening can help to minimize insect or pest attacks and protects the plants from excessive flooding when it rains heavily. It also works to keep the soil warm in early spring.

Think of a raised bed as a large container sitting on the ground with no base. It is a simple structure that is elegant and can be constructed to suit your decorative preferences. It is a cute addition to any space despite being a functional area for growing veggies and all types of ornamental plants, with a shocking degree of effectiveness.

Raised beds are supplied with quality soil of preference while keeping in mind all the determining factors like your choice of plants. Here, you are in complete control of all the conditions required for individual varieties.

Designs for Raised Bed Gardening

Raised garden beds can be constructed in a variety of shapes, sizes, looks, and designs. You can choose the portable kind or the fixed kind that can be permanently constructed in your garden or preferred space. They can be constructed with plastic, galvanized iron sheets, wood, or recycled brick stone. It is also possible to build a DIY raised bed with scrap materials readily available at home and at your desired height to achieve both design novelty and convenience.

If you are usually too busy or don't have the required space to pursue your gardening interests, raised bed gardening is the best alternative for you. It can be constructed to fit into your available space and is productive enough to give you contentment and pride in your gardening abilities. A bountiful harvest is expected even at the first attempt. If you're a kitchen gardener, a raised bed will be your secret weapon.

Benefits of Raised Bed Gardening

1. Instantly improved soil: Do you battle with clay-ridden soil or other undesirable soil conditions? Instead of wasting many farming seasons trying to fix your soil, you can simply create an almost perfect cultivating environment instantly with this gardening method. Placing your raised bed on the ground and filling it with high-quality soil is the solution you've been looking for. With accessible and loose soil, maintaining good cultivation conditions will be a breeze.

2. More productivity: Many gardeners have attested to the ability of raised beds to produce twice as much yield as ground beds; plants thrive in rich, loose soil that allows their roots to penetrate with ease.

There is also the benefit of good drainage and aeration. Raised beds prevent soil compression and ensure that the nutrient-rich soil amendments are in place and concentrated for crop nourishment. This promotes dense planting, which leads to more plants in less space than in-ground beds.

3. Longer cultivating season: Soil above ground stays better drained and warmer, thereby extending the growing season.

4. Efficient space: Most raised beds range from three to four feet wide in size, which makes them a great choice for the urban gardener and perfect for small spaces, which allows you to reach all your plants without having to stretch too far or step in. It also enables you to take full advantage of all the planting space.

5. Provision of plant protection: Your plants stay safely away from the annoying threat of human feet and pets.

6. Provision of pest barrier: Raised beds provide a sturdy defense against pests with a plant-based diet, such as snails and slugs. Tall sides guard against non-burrowing critters, and blockades like a hardware cloth can be kept underneath to prevent burrowing root-eating pests from getting to your plants.

7. Less emergence of weeds: Gardening with raised beds results in densely planted crops, which leaves little room for the growth of weeds. Many gardeners fortify this anti-weed fort by placing a weed barrier fabric underneath the bed. If weeds make it into your garden, they will be easy to remove because of the looseness of the soil.

8. Ease of accessibility: Ground beds are associated with a lot of bending, which has been eliminated by raised beds. Bye-bye backaches. The sides can be constructed to allow you to sit down while harvesting or tending to your crops.

9. Aesthetics: Raised beds also serve as an added architectural component because they can be built to be visually appealing. They can also create boundaries, focal points, and symmetry.

The Ideal Size for a Raised Bed

Several factors dictate the size of a raised bed, such as space limitations, physical convenience, and soil conditions; however, it all comes down to two things. Let's take a look at them.

1. Width and length: Mapping out the dimensions of the frame, first consider the constraints of the garden's space, which also includes room to walk around the raised bed. The second thing to consider is accessibility. You should be able to reach the center of your garden from both sides without the need to compress the soil. For some people, this means restricting the width to no more than 4 feet. If accessibility is limited to one side, restrict the width to about 3 feet. The length of your raised bed can be limited only by the lack of building materials and garden space.

2. Height: Most raised beds can be as high as 6 inches to 12 inches, or even 36 inches. The height depends mostly on how bad the underlying soil is. The worse it is, the deeper the bed should be to increase the amount of good soil provided to plants. Also, the deeper the soil, the better the root development. Deeper beds can contain more soil, which automatically means more moisture, which will reduce the time needed to water the plants.

The Varieties of Raised Bed Gardens

There are different kinds of raised beds in existence, including raised bed kits that can be purchased in the market. These kits can be constructed completely out of recycled plastic, cedar, composite wood, and galvanized steel. There are also raised bed designs that are elevated, which will save you the stress of bending every time you need to tend to your plants.

There are raised bed options that last longer. They can be constructed in mere minutes and last for a long time. These kinds are made of composite or recycled wood and usually sport a fancy cedar appearance. Kits like these will not splinter or rot, but if the goal is permanence, the raised bed should be constructed with stone or concrete.

Raised garden beds can be constructed to different heights, the least usually being 6 inches. While deciding on the perfect height for yourself, remember that more height equals more depth, and that means more soil, which will give the roots more room to grow. Usually, the roots of garden crops can grow to about 12 inches, so remember that. Deeper beds also retain more moisture for a longer time than shallow beds, which means you won't have to water the plants as often as in-ground beds.

If you have any issues bending over, it is suggested to use waist-high garden beds. Just remember that these beds consume a lot of compost and topsoil, and it can be a little expensive, but it will give you the chance to continue gardening without the concern of needing medication afterwards.

Ready-Made Raised Beds

A ready-made raised bed is one of the easiest things to assemble. You need only to unpack it, pour in soil, and start cultivating. There are different designs for raised beds in this category so ensure that you select ones that come in a convenient height, are big or small enough for your available space, and complement the existing style of your space.

- Ready-made metal raised beds: If you would like to give your garden a retro look, these pre-made metal beds fit the description. They are usually created from aluzinc steel panels, with stabilized safety edging and stainless-steel fasteners. They can be found in a variety of shapes and sizes, and are great for planting cut flowers and annual vegetables. They complement a balcony outside the kitchen door or even the patio.

- Wooden raised tables: These raised beds are perfect if you want to increase the height of your crops but don't want to fill the entire raised bed with soil. They work great for short-term annual crops that possess shallow root runs like salad crops. They have also proven productive with strawberries, reducing the risk of pests like snails and slugs. They are a nice addition to patios, balconies, and small gardens. They also come with an ease of maintenance and the most comfortable height to work at without straining your back. You'll mostly find them in dimensions like 4 by 4 feet or 2 by 4 feet, and 1 or 2 feet in depth. Most tables are constructed with a thick non-woven polypropylene fabric liner to help with water retention and ensure the durability of the timber.

• Raised trough beds: These are almost like raised wooden tables in that they both provide a comfortable height. They are also called mangers and come in a variety of sizes. The one advantage over wooden tables is the extra depth provided by raised beds. This means you can cultivate deeper rooted plants like parsnips and carrots. The outer, shallower edges can be used to plant shallow rooting vegetables. A liner should be placed on the sides and base of the inside to help retain water and shield the wood from damage.

The majority of pre-made troughs come with a three-year guarantee. A trough is great for small spaces like balconies or courtyards. Placing it close to the kitchen enables easy and quick harvesting of herbs and salad crops.

DIY Kits

Everyone enjoys a good DIY once in a while, especially ones as simple as self-assembly raised beds. They are built in a variety of sizes and shapes to suit different budgets so let's consider the options.

Wooden board kits: This is the most popular type of raised bed kits. They are a great value for your cash and are built in many widths and lengths to give a reasonable degree of garden flexibility. Wooden boards are generally 6 inches in depth, but can also be obtained in 8 inches. They are about five tiers tall, so five 6-inch-deep wooden boards guarantee a 2.5-foot-tall, raised bed. This is a comfortable height for gardeners in wheelchairs.

The wood used usually comes in different types according to quality, but it is commonly built with Scandinavian softwood treated with a non-toxic preservative. It comes with a thickness that ranges from ¾ to 1.5 inches to ensure a sturdy structure that withstands the weight of the soil. A wooden board is great because it is fitted with hoops and covers to protect the plants from pests and frost.

Wooden corner beds: These are the smaller version of the wooden raised beds, which makes them perfect for people with small spaces. They can fit into the tiniest of spaces, thereby increasing the number of vegetables that can be cultivated in the back of the garden. Like the wooden boards, they are available in a variety of sizes and heights.

Hugelkultur: This is a northern European horticultural concept, and its popularity is on the rise as more people are searching for self-sustaining garden methods, lessening the need for constant feeding and watering of the plants. It is a system that depends on the decomposition of wood. This kind of raised bed garden works like a sponge, withholding and releasing nutrients and moisture when necessary.

Hugelkultur involves placing rotting logs, sticks, and branches on top of each other to form piles, and layering soil over them so they resemble little hills. The tops and sides are then used to plant crops. The hills can be built to be large by burying entire tree trunks and leaving them to decompose, or small by burying only a bundle of sticks.

How to Build

1. Remove the turf from your preferred location. Preserve the sod.

2. Dig the underlying soil until it is 12 inches deep. Preserve the soil, separating the subsoil from the topsoil.

3. Place rotting and unrotting timber and logs in the pit to form a pile, with the largest forming the base.

4. Stack the wood until you reach your preferred height.

5. Place the turf over the pile of logs and top with subsoil. Make sure to get some soil between the gaps in the wood.

6. Layer the top and sides with compost or topsoil. Use a rake or your hands to sculpt the soil to form a mound shape. Place logs at the edges to keep surrounding weeds from creeping into your garden bed.

Keyhole Raised Garden Bed

The keyhole garden bed has its origins in Africa, but it is now a worldwide horticultural concept. It is a circular raised bed with a notch cut out for accessibility and maintenance. From a bird's eye view, it is shaped like a keyhole, hence its name. Right in the middle is a compost bin that can be reached through the notch. This compost bin works to supply the surrounding soil with moisture and nutrients.

Due to the compact size of the structure, wires can create frameworks over the bed, which are used to train runner beans, sweet peas, and other climbing plants. They also function as support for shade cloths or netting during hot weather.

The outside walls were traditionally made with stones and rocks in Africa due to their abundance and ability to absorb warmth in the daytime. However, bricks, lumber, empty paint pots filled with soil, and corrugated metal are being used today as building blocks for the garden wall.

How to Build

1. Clear your preferred location, including space for movement around the bed. Remove all perennial weeds in sight.

2. Put a bamboo cane with a string tied to it at the midpoint of where the raised bed will be constructed, tie the other end of the

string to another bamboo cane with 5 feet between them. This guide will outline the 10-foot circular raised bed.

3. Make a notch in the circle. It should be roughly ⅛ of the total space.

4. Break up any compression by using a fork to dig over the soil. Then build the outer wall. The traditional height is approximately 3 feet, but it can be adjusted to suit personal preferences.

5. Now build a compost bin at the center of the garden. This is traditionally constructed by weaving flexible canes or sticks together. Bamboo and willow are perfect choices. However, it is much easier to form a tube with a wire mesh or chicken wire, creating a diameter of 2 feet and a height of 4 feet. Keep it secured by pushing bamboo canes through the mesh.

6. Use straw or cardboard to line the insides of the external wall, then layer it with moist biodegradable material.

7. Place alternative layers of green and brown waste board materials like kitchen scraps and cardboard to the compost bin. They will ensure that your plants get the necessary nutrients and moisture. Make sure not to fill it to the brim to leave space for new materials.

8. Your raised bed garden is now ready for use. Try not to water the plants too regularly. This will force the roots deeper into the center of the bed, making them self-reliant.

Woven Raised Bed Gardens

This raised bed design is great for cottage gardens and is a beautiful feature all by itself. Using supple branches to build structures is one of the oldest methods of construction.

How to Build

1. Clear your preferred location of unwanted materials, and mark the shape of the bed on the ground using string, flour, or sand.

2. Drill wooden stakes into the ground using a sledgehammer to signify where the corners will be. Hazel stakes should also be placed every 20 inches along the sides. Oak, chestnut, and willow may be used. Char them over the fire briefly to make them harder and more durable.

3. Now weave some young willow branches between the posts; ensure it is tightly woven. Stop when the raised bed is high enough.

4. Line the inside of the wall with a black plastic sheet or horticultural fabric liner to extend the life of the branches by a few years.

Recycled Pallet Raised Beds

Pallets are great for recycling because the wood is durable and strong. They look a little rough, but they can be filed and painted to look funky or chic. If you are a DIY enthusiast, you can use the leftover pallets to make complementary benches, tables, and chairs. Note that this raised bed must be constructed.

How to Build

1. You will use four pallets of the same size to form the sides of the bed. If you need to reduce the height of the pallets, don't forget to wear gloves when sawing.

2. Two or three more pallets will be required. Remove the slats from there using a crowbar.

3. Place the first four pallets on the ground and screw the slats over the gaps.

4. Place the four pallets upright and hold them together by screwing metal corner brackets. You should have a box shape when you're done.

5. To protect the sides from rot, line the insides with a plastic sheet or landscape fabric.

6. Give the edges an attractive finish by attaching extra slats to the top edges.

7. File the outside of the box and paint it whatever color you'd like, using an exterior undercoat before exterior wood paint.

8. When the paint has dried, pour in your soil and compost, and it's ready for use.

Recycled Materials

One person's treasure can be another person's trash. You can use almost anything to construct a raised bed, and most of these materials are very affordable or free, environment-friendly, and very fashionable. With recycled materials, you can create looks that range from shabby chic to bohemian, making it seem like you hired expensive garden designers to give your space a makeover. The materials you can use include:

Trash cans: Metal trash cans and old plastic cans are a great option for raised bed construction. About four drainage holes should be made in the bottom and the cans filled with compost to make an ideal cultivating bed.

Old bathtubs: Know any local builders? Contact them for old metal or tin bathtubs from houses that underwent renovation. Simply fill them with soil and get planting.

Old wheelbarrows: No need to trash an old wheelbarrow when you can transform it into the most productive garden. It makes a stylish mini-bed which can be moved around easily. You have only to drill a few holes at the bottom for drainage and fill the barrow with high-quality compost.

Old boats and scrap cars: Raised garden beds can even be constructed from old scrap cars, as shocking as it may sound. Simply pour enough compost into the hoods or trunks, or inside the bodies if you are dealing with a convertible. If the windows and windshields are okay, the inside of the car should make a great greenhouse.

Builder bags: Large builder bags, also called bulk bags, are a fantastic material for the construction of raised beds for many reasons. They are very mobile, easily obtainable, free, incredibly porous, and are an aesthetic addition to the garden. Bulk bags are the large white bags used by builders to transport materials like gravel, compost, and topsoil to building sites and domestic houses. You can use them as they are or construct a wooden frame around them to give them more support and beauty. Simply place them at the desired location and fill with soil.

Rooftop Gardens

These must be ultimately raised beds. They are the perfect solution for the urban gardener without a lot of garden space and a colorful and productive addition to any building. They also attract butterflies and pollinating bees and are a great makeover for unused space.

If you intend to build a rooftop garden you can walk into, consider how heavy the garden is relative to the roof structure. A structural engineer should do this math for accuracy. You will also review building regulations if you'd like to convert a window to a door for access to the garden. If you intend to make any structural changes to the roof, and of course with the actual gardening, you may need to get planning permission as it may affect the privacy of the surrounding neighbors.

Suppose your building doesn't have a flat roof for roof gardening, no need to throw away your gardening interests. There are outdoor staircases in apartments that are laden with containers filled with plants, great as long as they do not obstruct the fire escape in times of emergency. Window boxes are also excellent for raised bed gardening in the absence of a flat roof. The kitchen window is a great suggestion for your window boxes, especially if you intend to cultivate edible crops.

How to Build

Simply select aesthetic containers that complement the current style of the building. A traditional terracotta or aluminum is ideal for a modern house.

Green Roof Garden Beds

Green roofs have become extremely popular as more people are interested in beautifying urban spaces and towns. They help to fight poor air quality and pollution and, like roof gardens, they are a great way to utilize unused space. They may also attract relatively harmless wildlife, which is a huge bonus for animal lovers.

How to Build

1. The first thing to do is get a structural engineer to determine if the building can withstand the weight of the garden.

2. Take measurements of your roof and cut a marine sheet to its exact size.

3. Line the marine plywood with black sheeting or butyl liner and place it on the roof.

4. 3-inch cleats should now be attached to the outer edges of the plywood to form a shallow cultivating frame.

5. Now pour in a mix of general-purpose soil, rock wool, and perlite. This will make the compost substrate lighter than usual to lessen the weight on the roof. The depth depends on the plant you want to cultivate.

6. Make holes for drainage at the bottom edge of the baton to ensure that the bed doesn't become waterlogged. Ensure that you plug the drains with rock wool in the rainy season to prevent your cultivating medium from being washed out.

Chapter Two: Pros and Cons of Raised Bed Gardening

Everything, no matter how seemingly perfect, has pros and cons-including raised bed gardening. It is time to consider the advantages and disadvantages of this method of gardening. We will begin with the notable pros of using raised beds, which includes the advantages they have over ground beds. Several perks are undeniable; however, a few others are slightly more relative, like style and aesthetics. Regardless, raised beds are a popular and great way to grow food comfortably at home. Let's consider why.

The Pros of Raised Bed Gardening

You possess control over the quality of your soil: Raised bed gardening gives you total control over the quality, texture, and condition of your soil. Instead of simply settling for what you have, it is possible to fill your raised bed with a high-quality soil that your plants will thank you for. Soil composition and quality are considered one of the most vital factors in successful gardening.

The best soil for gardening is rich with organic substances, will readily retain water, but also drains well and has a loose texture that easily allows for root growth. This describes the best soil type for farming, sandy loam. Healthy soil also contains some important microorganisms which may not be present in the soil you already have.

Many urban gardeners find their soil undesirable or unsuitable for cultivating food for many reasons. For instance, the soil might have a crummy composition or poor drainage and will need a lot of time, attention, and work for amendment before planting. Also, the soil may have been formerly treated with pesticides or herbicides, which led to contamination.

Some native soils may also be extremely silty. Silty soil lacks air pockets to encourage microbial life, water retention, and structure unless enough effort is put in to saturate it thoroughly. Raised bed gardening gives you the chance to create your perfect growing environment for planting with no need to wait for a long time or put in an exhausting amount of effort.

Determining depth: Raised beds tend to be deep enough for plants that need ample space for their roots. Deeper and bigger root systems mean more yummy plants. This benefit, however, will vary according to how deep you'd like to construct your beds and the structures you install them on, if any.

Generally, it is recommended to stick to a minimum depth of one-foot-tall, raised beds. Raised beds are blocked by a solid bottom or weed barrier fabric. It is advised to construct beds with a minimum depth of 18 inches. Certain plants will thrive in not-so-deep soil, but the most common garden plants–like peppers, eggplants, kale, and tomatoes–will require much deeper soil. Deeper raised beds also have great moisture retention and are better shielded from flooding than ground beds.

This does not mean that ground beds are incapable of having deep soil. However, the composition of the soil might be an issue regardless of depth. Great soil depth without equally great soil composition won't create an ideal growing condition for your plants.

Raised beds are more convenient: Many gardeners usually prefer raised beds because of how comfortable they are compared to ground gardens, especially for their knees and backs. They are easily accessible for gardeners who use a walker or wheelchair or simply have issues stooping or bending. You might need to get on your knees sometimes with some raised beds, but that can be done with a padded kneeler, and you will be less hunched over. As I mentioned earlier, raised beds can be constructed to your desired height, so bending or kneeling can become a thing of the past.

Also, if your mobility is limited or you suffer back issues, it is recommended to construct your raised beds no wider than three or four feet and as long as you'd like. A wider bed will require more bending and leaning to reach the center. There are also raised beds mounted on legs for even more comfort.

Raised beds are mostly pest-proof: Cultivating edible or ornamental plants in raised garden beds ensures an added protective layer against pests. The height of the bed and frame both serve as effective barriers and potential discouragement for plant-eating pests like rabbits, slugs, and snails unless they're determined to eat your garden. Regardless, it isn't difficult to add floating row covers and hoops to block them completely. This has also proven effective against birds, neighborhood cats, squirrels, skunks, and much more.

Netted row covers and hoops can keep pests away from ground beds, but not the kinds that burrow through the soil. For this reason, raised beds are considered a lifesaver by many gardeners. Gophers are a real issue because it is almost impossible to cultivate food in ground beds without gophers killing or eating them. Depending on how they are constructed, raised beds can stop destructive pests, like moles, voles and gophers from destroying your plants.

The bottom of your raised bed can be lined with galvanized hardware cloth to protect your crops. You can also make DIY hardware cloth gopher baskets if you are planning to plant fruit trees. This method protects your plants without requiring you to engage in a never-ending battle by endlessly purchasing traps and poisons to deal with pests.

It is also possible to construct your raised bed high enough to discourage chickens or dogs. Chicken wire is more affordable and mostly used rather than hardware cloth to make gopher baskets or line the base of raised beds. I don't recommend chicken wire, because it tends to disintegrate over time, and it can be chewed through by certain pests. Hardware cloth is a better option for raised beds in areas where burrowing pests are a hazard.

Less weed growth: Raised beds also have the benefit of reducing weed intrusion, unlike ground beds. First, raised beds that have been filled with fresh weed-free soil are very unlikely to grow any weeds, unlike ground beds and native soil that may contain weed seeds and weeds themselves.

The height of the borders in raised beds keeps weeds from creeping into your garden from the surrounding pathways. It is also possible to install a weed barrier at the bottom to keep invasive weeds from creeping into your beds. This must be done before adding soil, or the purpose will be defeated. Weed barriers include cardboard, weed barrier fabric, and so on.

If the preferred location for your raised bed is slightly weedy, before installation, line the bottom with unwaxed cardboard to help kill most or all weeds. Despite the effectiveness of cardboard, some situations require methods that are more effective and durable. Commercial-duty landscape fabric will keep weeds, especially crabgrass, from getting comfortable in your raised beds.

Raised beds are really beautiful. This does not mean that ground beds are not aesthetically appealing; however, the extra visual interest created by raised beds is simply gold. They can create dimension and a well-structured cultivating area. Planter containers of various heights, shapes, and sizes can be organized to create attractive and unique garden designs. Wood planter boxes are also beautiful even when they aren't growing anything, especially if they are wrapped in solar string lights.

It is relatively easy to maintain the aesthetics of a raised bed garden, unlike ground beds. Their borders and edges keep pathway ground cover like bark mulch or gravel from spilling into the garden itself.

They can be placed anywhere: Raised beds can be placed in a variety of locations. Just like containers and other pits, raised beds are very adaptable, with a few being mobile. Ground beds are fixed, so they are limited to only their current location, and that may or may not receive proper sunlight or be level.

Raised beds can be added to a balcony, patio area, terraced into the side of a slope or hill, or even constructed on a rooftop. Technically, they can be created anywhere with good exposure and sound structure. For example, you can construct a few raised beds in your driveway during spring because it receives the greatest amount of sun in the afternoon.

If you plan to set up a raised bed on top of a solid surface, like a balcony or patio, you need to consider adequate drainage, critical for every good, raised bed. The bed also should be constructed with some kind of bottom to keep the soil in place. If not, the soil will seep out slowly, creating a mess you don't want to deal with. One way to do this is to line the open base with geotextile fabric, or you can simply choose a fabric raised bed or a bulk bag.

The Cons of Raised Bed Gardening

As can be seen, there are many respectable pros of raised bed gardening. However, certain potential drawbacks are worth placing under consideration. Let's look at some of the notable ones.

Raised beds require upfront cost and more materials: If only stylish raised garden beds appeared out of thin air. Unfortunately, that is not the case. Tools, lumber, a huge amount of high-quality soil, and screws are required to bring this method of gardening to life. The cost of healthy soil and necessary materials can pile up, especially if you are constructing and filling multiple beds simultaneously. Ground garden beds are more affordable and simpler, and although you might still need to purchase certain amendments and compost before getting started, it is nowhere near as much as that needed for raised beds.

One of the few ways to ensure that filling your raised bed is more economical than usual is to purchase compost and quality soil in bulk. You can also build your gardens and install raised beds in stages, dealing with mini-projects over a while to spread out the cost. Another effective way to do this is to embrace the increasingly popular method of hugelkultur. All you will need is space, branches, bark, and/or logs from anywhere around your property.

Raised beds require a good amount of handy basic skills: If you plan to build your raised bed from scratch, you will need to have certain tools, skills, and physical strength. You will also be required to know basic calculations to purchase the correct sizes and amount of materials and design the garden. If you do not own a saw, lumber departments may cut the boards to your preferred length for you. If it's your first raised bed and you find you don't own a power drill, you might need to resort to nailing it together by hand, though I do not recommend it.

Setting up a ground bed garden also requires a bit of muscle as well, but it is not as tasking and more straightforward, requiring next to zero amount of tools. Fortunately, putting together the parts of a rectangular box is one of the most straightforward and simple DIY projects that can be done by almost anyone, so don't be spooked. To simplify things there are step-by-step tutorial videos all over the internet explaining how to set up your raised bed kit. If you don't feel up to constructing your own from scratch or purchasing a kit, there are pre-made raised beds on the market for convenience. They are available in many sizes, heights, and depths.

They are not eternal: Unfortunately, your raised bed will need to be repaired or be entirely replaced, unlike ground garden beds.

When it is time for repairs, a lot of work will be required to replace wooden boards, move the soil, or simply change the entire bed and its contents. Fortunately, the lifespan of a raised bed depends on the material it is built with. For instance, raised beds made of bricks or stones will be more durable than beds made of wood or bulk bags. Also, properly-made wooden boxes will last far longer than poorly made ones.

It is always advisable to build raised beds from good quality wood that is at least 2 inches thick like heart redwood or cedar, which are not only termite- and rot-resistant but can last for more than a decade. Heart redwood is easily obtainable on the west coast and is just as cheap as cedar, which is readily available on the east coast. Redwood and cedar are more expensive than Douglas fir, fence boards, cheap pinewood, repurposed scrap wood, thin 1-inch boards, and plywood. However, they are prone to bow and rot. Also, stay away from pressure-treated lumber because they are packed with toxins, especially if you intend to grow edible plants. The cost of high-quality wood is worth the investment when planning a raised bed garden.

Raised beds are not temporary: When you construct or install your raised garden bed, it is a little difficult to alter the layout of your garden space or change the location of beds. This doesn't mean it is impossible to do; it is simply relatively difficult. You will need to dig out the soil to relocate or redesign them, and that can be a lot of work, especially if convenience was one of the major reasons you started raised bed gardening. Bagging up soil and moving wood from one location to another can be a very tiring experience. Compared to raised beds, ground beds can be easily modified without as much effort. All you simply must do is dig up a new space. You can even plow it over and reseed the area if you like.

You may have limited curves and shapes: Maybe you prefer to enjoy the feel of a more flowing, soft, and natural garden. Ground bed gardens leave room for more flexibility with design and creative shapes, forming fewer hard lines than raised garden beds.

Planter boxes are often limited to rectangular or square shapes unless you own the right tools and are handy. However, it is possible to add some softness and flow to your raised bed garden space in a few ways. For instance, if you have cobblestone-bordered cultivating areas, you can plant flowers, billowing shrubs, and construct curved pathways to give balance to the structure.

So, there you have it! The benefits and potential setbacks of raised bed gardening. As you must have noticed, the potential pros of this method of gardening depend largely on your native soil, aesthetic preferences, unique garden space, the prevalence of pests, and the budget. For many gardeners, the benefits of cultivating with a raised garden bed greatly outweigh the cons, despite both gardening styles being wonderful and worthy.

Chapter Three: Selecting Materials and Styles for Raised Beds

Raised bed gardening is becoming increasingly popular, as mentioned earlier, and for good reasons. People are quickly turning back to nature as a source of safe, reliable, cheap, and healthy food. Its popularity has led to innovations, and these innovations have led countless blogs to feature countless construction materials for raised bed gardening. However, not every featured material is suitable for this method of gardening, with some being very harmful to you and your soil if you are not informed.

Materials to Stay Away From in Raised Bed Gardening

Recycling is generally eco-friendly, and in some cases, is an ideal choice for raised bed construction. However, certain recycled materials must be avoided when trying to construct your raised beds.

Railroad ties: This material has been used to build staircases, garden beds, and other landscape constructs all over the United

States. Despite its popularity and availability, it does not look worth the cost, especially if you peer deeper into how the wood was chemically treated before it was ready for use.

The most important aspect of these chemical treatments is creosote and its uses. Creosote has been confirmed to be made of over 300 different chemicals, a lot of which are potentially dangerous to humans and can contaminate the surrounding soil. The EPA has issued several warning announcements against the use of railroad ties in any kind of landscape construction, so you should stay away from it, even if you like the way it looks.

Tires: Tires are usually used for growing potatoes or as a creative way to spice up the look of a garden. This has been beneficial by keeping tires out of the landfill. However, there are heavy metals in these tires. These metals can leach into the surrounding soil, contaminating any food being cultivated on them. There have been arguments about the rubber in tires acting as a binding agent, keeping the metals from separating from the tires and contaminating the soil. At any rate, if you are intent on using tires in your garden, for your own safety ensure that you only plant inedible flowers.

Pallets: Pallets are a great material to use in constructing raised beds as long as you are aware of their source. Pallets were originally meant for shipping materials and had the remainders of whatever they transported. Some pallets have also been treated with methyl bromide, an infamous disruptive chemical that can negatively affect endocrine health. A lot of pallet manufacturers quit the use of the chemical in 2005; however, there are still many old pallets in circulation. If you must use a pallet in your garden, always search for a stamp that says "heat-treated" or "HT." If you don't find a stamp or cannot verify if it has been heat-treated, don't use it.

Treated lumber: A lot of gardeners, including the experienced ones, rely on treated lumber when in need of materials for raised bed construction because of its extra protection against rot, bug damage, and moisture. True, treated lumber is more durable than other materials for the same purpose, but it can also release toxins into the soil, contaminating your food.

Over the years, pressure-treated lumber has been developed with chromate copper arsenate, which eventually leaches arsenic into the soil. Most lumber producers today have stopped the use of CCA during processing. Instead, alkaline copper quat and copper azole are being used, and despite not being as toxic, copper can find its way into your soil, which won't be organic.

If your raised bed has been constructed with pressure-treated wood, make sure to give your plants enough phosphorus via your compost. Plants have a higher chance of absorbing arsenic if they live in phosphorus-deficient soil.

The Best Material for Raised Bed Construction

Heart redwood or cedar: Redwood and cedar stylishly enhance the look of your garden while guaranteeing you a natural resistance to bugs, rot, and moisture. These materials will break down with time, but you can enjoy five or more years from a well-built redwood or cedar bed, with a few even surviving for more than a decade.

Cedar lumber is usually used by experienced gardeners in constructing raised beds and for good reasons. It is naturally resistant to insects and rot. Juniperus virginiana, also called Eastern red cedar, is very resistant to rot and is extremely durable even in the soil. The only downside is that the wood can be difficult to work with because of its density. Eastern red cedar is difficult to find, especially in bulk, because it isn't manufactured locally. It can also be very costly.

Thuja plicata, also known as west coast cedar, is not as difficult to work with, although it tends to split when wood screws are used without pre-drilling. It is easily obtainable compared to other kinds of cedar. There are a few concerns about the sustainability of its production practices. Also, a lot of fuel is required to transport it because of the location of its production. It is about five times more expensive than Southern yellow pine but is usually well worth the investment.

Cypress: This type of wood is native to the southeast and easily obtainable in Georgia compared to cedar, although it usually cannot be purchased at discount lumber stores. It is resistant to insects and rot, especially when in contact with soil. It is more durable than regular pine. It might be a little difficult and expensive to order from a lumber store, but if it is grown and milled in your region, it is much cheaper and a preferred alternative to cedar.

Pine: This has its origins in the southeast, and it is the most readily available lumber in Georgia. Southern yellow pine is one of the easiest and strongest woods to use in construction. It is also very affordable and can be obtained in a variety of grades, with the highest grade being the least common and obviously the best. Regardless of the grade, pine has little to no resistance to insects and rot. Its lifespan is shortened when used in close contact with soil. The only pines exempted from this are the ones from very old buildings. Forty-year-old pine wood is amazingly sturdy, dense, and straight compared to modern-day pine. When seeking pine for the construction of your raised bed, reclaim wood from older buildings and barns because they are a great alternative and more organic compared to other building materials.

Hardwoods like oak: Hardwoods are a little hard to obtain in large sizes or quantities, and according to research, they are only slightly better at resisting insects and rot than pine. The cost of some hardwoods is a prohibiting factor. They are also generally difficult to work with after they have dried up.

Organic Wood Preservatives

Commercial wood preservatives have been put under intense scrutiny in the past decade, especially creosote and the other copper-based pressure-treated lumber, like the green stained lumber used in constructing decks. As I mentioned earlier, recycled wooden utility poles and railroad ties should be avoided when constructing raised beds that will be used to grow edible food due to their treatment with creosote. Similar concerns have been brought forward about pressure-treated lumber, although certain modern formulations seem safe for the production of food.

Regardless, USDA Organic Certification guidelines forbid the use of any pressure-treated lumber to be used in direct contact with edible plants. That means we are stuck with relatively few options for treating lumber for raised garden beds. The two most popular products for this purpose are tung oil and linseed oil. They are not only organic but have also been proven to extend the life of wood even in direct contact with soil.

Linseed oil: This is a flaxseed extract that can shield natural wooden products from rot. It is vital to understand the difference between boiled linseed oil and raw linseed oil. Boiled linseed oil is a combination of raw linseed oil and artificial solvents that may not be safe to use in organic systems. Raw linseed oil is a very affordable natural wood preservative. It is not as effective as copper-based preservatives or creosote, but it is completely organic. Note that linseed oil is a source of food for mildew, so don't be surprised when you see mildew growth on wood preserved with linseed oil.

Tung oil: This is a tung tree extract that has proven effective in the preservation of wood. It is more expensive than linseed oil and is usually mixed with toxic solvents that help in application and absorption.

Unpreserved Wood

This kind of lumber makes some of the most beautiful, homey looking pieces, including raised beds. The one thing to remember, however, is that products made from untreated wood are not as durable as the other options. Raised beds made with untreated wood can work for about three years before they need replacing. This has proven itself to be a good economical option for gardeners looking for cheap, durable, and temporary raised beds before making some permanent raised bed additions to the garden.

Rocks

If rocks can be easily obtained from around your property, make good use of them by building a natural raised bed. You might exhaust yourself trying to get the rocks to the preferred location. Still, the initial effort will produce long-term benefits, considering rock raised beds are almost eternal, requiring little maintenance. You will also need mortar to glue the rocks together, at least while building upwards for height.

Remember that this option is only economical if you already have rocks around your property. Buying rocks will only result in more cost and is inadvisable unless you intend to do it more for pure aesthetics than function.

Bricks

This is another stylish option but can be a little pricey depending on the brick you're in the market for, whether recycled or new. Just like rocks, gardens made with bricks last for many decades, requiring little maintenance. A cheaper alternative has gathered a lot of attention recently, thanks to YouTube-cement blocks. However, do not use the cinder block form of cement blocks, particularly the older ones, if they are mixed with fly ash. Contained within fly ash are arsenic, lead, mercury, and so on, which will seep into the surrounding soil and contaminate your food.

Concrete Blocks

These are the cheapest and easiest material to use to construct a raised bed garden. Cement blocks are readily available for free or a little fee. They can be placed on top of each other to make fairly high raised beds. However, if the walls are higher than two levels, use mortar to hold them together to prevent collapse. It is easier to find cement blocks that have been used, but remember that stacking used blocks without mortar is almost impossible.

Pots and Containers

This is a great option for gardeners who live in apartments but are still interested in pursuing their gardening interests. Even gardeners with ample space can reap the benefits from the pots placed in nooks and crannies of abandoned space. This is especially perfect for spreading plants, like certain caneberries and mint, in bigger pots. Don't forget to drill extra holes than those provided by the manufacturer for better drainage.

When purchasing pots for planting, seek ones that are BPA-free to keep BPA from seeping into the soil. This information is usually found at the bottom of the pot.

Composite Wood

Composite wood is becoming increasingly popular for outdoor building projects due to its durability and relative ease of use. It is made of a mixture of pulp or wood fibers and plastic resins and is then shaped in different dimensions of lumber. It is expensive and available in a few basic sizes, especially ones for decking. Typically, it is about three to four times the cost of basic treated pinewood.

The lifespan of composite wood in direct contact with soil hasn't been confirmed. Studies of the effects of composite wood for decking have shown that the wood undergoes many kinds of deterioration similar to traditional wood such as discoloration, mildew, cracking, degradation in light, and mold. Studies have also confirmed that composite wood has more environmental costs than pine or cedar.

Mortared Walls

Mortared walls are a more permanent and more secure construct. Dry stacked walls are not as expensive, easier to set up but also not as permanent. Concrete excavated from sidewalks and driveways is usually obtainable for free. If you get tiny pieces in a uniform thickness, you can use them as great recycled materials for your raised bed walls. There are certain areas in Georgia where granite rubble is easily obtained. If they are angular stones, they can be stacked into walls. Keep in mind that a stone wall cannot be constructed higher than a single level, with mortar to keep the stones together.

Raised Bed Kits

These have gained popularity at local garden centers and with internet suppliers. Often, they make raised bed construction fast and easy. They are typically made of either western cedar or cheap plastic, and while some kits only contain the hardware, others are the entire package. The quality and variety of raised bed kits vary greatly, so be cautious when making purchases, ensuring that you know of the kit you want before a purchase is made.

Regardless of the size of your garden space, raised beds are the perfect organic solution for cultivating healthy and productive crops at any skill level and age. As long as you make use of the right materials for safety, convenience, and style preference, you will be on the path to a more active, healthy, and self-sufficient lifestyle.

Chapter Four: Creating a Layout Plan for Your Space

A functional planting scheme needs a good plan. More time should be allotted to choosing and selecting the proper crops than the main process of cultivating. You must decide on the style you require and then research the plants' requirements.

Raised beds are an efficient way of gardening, but they come with a list of challenges. Proper planning and an awareness of all the factors involved are necessary if you intend to have a functional raised bed garden.

Practical Things to Consider

Lifting certain materials to a certain height is considered hard work by some, even to the point of causing injury or strain if done incorrectly. For instance, a watering can is very convenient when watering plants at a relatively low height, while lifting the same can to a raised bed height can feel uncomfortable. Thankfully, solutions to this exist in a hose or an irrigation system.

It is not easy to lift heavy materials like heavy plants or wheelbarrow loads of compost. However, there are solutions such as scaffold boards or low ramps to help push the compost in little amounts onto wheelbarrows. Or you can always use lighter, smaller containers like buckets to move building materials.

The Perfect Height

There are tall climbing crops like hops and French runner beans, which might grow too tall beyond reach if you cultivate them in upright structures or high raised beds. This will require the use of a ladder to tend to and harvest your crops. Luckily, there are shorter versions of these plants just as productive and easy to grow. Always keep height in consideration.

The Budget

The cost of constructing a raised bed is higher than planting in-ground beds, regardless of the kind of materials you intend to use for construction-whether rocks, lumber, or bricks-unless you have enough of these materials around your property. You also must purchase screws, drills, hammers, jigsaws, and nails to hold them together, and consider the cost of your planting material. If we lived in a perfect world, everyone would have their own bags of homemade compost, but most people will need to import soil and compost into the garden. One good thing is that the initial outlay is always worth the costs because, in time, the beds will become increasingly efficient, producing bountiful harvest every season. At least you won't have to spend money on pest control.

Moisture Retention

The kind of raised bed you finally settle on will determine if you must water the plants more often than you would in-ground beds. This is due to the better drainage provided by raised beds when compared to ground beds, which can be a good thing; however, some drain more than others. Raised beds like the keyhole garden and hugelkultur are designed to retain water instead of losing it.

The Drawing Board

The ideal way to start planning your raised bed design is to draw out the plan on a piece of paper, determining what plants will be placed where. This stage of the planning process saves you from making expensive mistakes, like purchasing more plants than you need from the garden center.

If you intend to plant veggies in your raised beds, then you will need to plot methodically to determine the appropriate position for each vegetable. This ensures that all plants are given the necessary space and prevents the smaller ones from constantly living in the shadow of the taller ones. During this process, you might find you need more than one raised bed so you can engage in crop rotation every year. If your garden is strictly ornamental, you will need to make sure that your preferred plants are suitable for the climate conditions and soil type.

Style: Pick a Color

For an ornamental raised bed, you will also take into consideration the color combinations of the plants. You may find you want a single-color theme in your garden, or you may wish to have colors that project a particular mood like tranquil, calming pastel colors, or vibrant, bright, hot colors. Many gardeners use a color wheel to determine the colors that will go well together.

The Color Wheel

A color wheel is an important tool for determining great color combinations. They are not only used in gardening but also in other areas like fashion, art, marketing, and so on. The rule is that the colors sitting alongside one another, like yellow and green, will be a calm and harmonious combination. In contrast, colors on the opposite sides of each other on the wheel, like purple and yellow, make a clashing combination and a striking impact.

The Importance of Size

When designing a ground garden bed, the placement rules are usually according to size and are fairly easy: The short plants stay in front while the tall ones stay at the back. However, raised beds are a little different because they can be viewed from multiple angles, so consider how you want the bed to be viewed.

If you construct a path that runs around the entirety of your raised bed, it will be seen from all angles, meaning that the shorter plants should be placed at the edges and the taller plants in the center. Remember that the taller plants might throw some shade on the shorter plants according to the movement of the sun, so carefully consider the position of all plants.

If you intend to grow vegetables, consider placing the shade-tolerant plants like lettuce and leafy veggies next to the taller vegetables. Keep sun-loving plants like pumpkins, squashes, and tomatoes close to the edges of the bed, away from the taller vegetables. Remember that plants such as potatoes and carrots require at least half a day of direct sunlight.

The Perfect Depth

Different raised beds require different depths for different reasons. These factors are determined by the plants you intend to grow and whether the bed is situated on a patio, has a board at the bottom, or is in direct contact with the soil below. If the bed sits directly on the soil, the crops with bigger roots will spread beyond the depth of the raised bed into the ground below. Here, the height of the raised bed is not important.

Annuals, Herbs, and Salad Crops

If you intend to grow only a handful of salad crops yearly, you will require a raised bed that is about 4 inches deep. Salad crops tend to have shallow roots and will even be equally productive in a window box, so depth in a raised bed is not a necessity. There are other reasons for wanting to use a higher raised bed besides depth, like aesthetics or ease of maintenance. Begonia, petunia, lobelia, annual rudbeckia, cosmos, Busy Lizzie, and other annual bedding crops require similar conditions and do not possess large root systems, meaning they are fine with shallow soil. Most perennial herbs like mint, thyme, and rosemary have their origins in the Mediterranean region, where they grew in rocky and arid soil conditions, so they will not require the depth.

Deep-Rooted Vegetables, Ornamental Grasses, and Herbaceous Perennials

Herbaceous crops require depth in raised beds because they typically have a larger root system than annual crops. Veggies like potatoes, peas, beans, carrots, cabbages, and so on also require depth. To be specific, a depth of at least 12 inches is required for them to reach their higher point of productivity. They can grow in shallow beds, but you might need to water and feed them more than usual to make up for the lack of depth.

Fruit Bushes and Shrubs

Many shrubs and fruit bushes need a depth of at least 20 inches to grow and develop to their full potential. Like deeper-rooted vegetables, they can grow in shallow soil, but they will be considerably stunted and are likely to have short lifespans compared to the same plants in deeper soil.

Trees

Did you know that when you look at a tree, the part you see above is usually a mirror of what is below in the form of root systems? Now imagine the root system of a huge tree. Remember that trees are typically adaptable, the bonsai tree being a good example of trees curtailing their growth to fit the available space. Certain trees can be purchased on dwarf rootstock, which curtails their overall size. In an ideal world, trees should be granted a depth of at least 3 to 4 feet in a raised bed.

Factors to Consider When Siting Your Raised Bed

One of the major keys to successful gardening is placing the right plants in the right raised bed relative to the position of the bed. If you are dealing with a small garden, you are unlikely to have a lot of options for siting your raised beds, but fortunately, plants for every aspect exist, whether it's a sunbaked, shady, dry, or damp corner bed.

Shady Corner Beds

If you can, and your space allows it, the best site for your raised bed is an open, sunny area. Most plants thrive in maximum sunlight; the more sun exposure to their leaves, the higher their production of sugars, which sweetens any vegetable or fruit they produce. However, if your space doesn't permit you to place your raised bed in direct sunlight for most of the day, no worries because there are plants that love the shade. Leafy plants like spinach, summer salad greens, and cabbages like it cooler. Shady corners mean that the beds are less likely to dry out due to a lot of sun exposure, and the vegetables have less tendency to bolt because they enjoy the cool root system. Many ornamental plants also thrive in shady corners, like ferns, hellebores, Epimedium, and hostas.

Proper Lighting

Before constructing a raised bed, it is advisable to find the area where the sunlight touches the most to maximize the sunlight given to your plants. This might seem obvious but remember that a flower planted directly on a ground bed, especially in small gardens, might be blocked from direct sunlight when elevated onto a raised bed. Walls, roofs, and tree canopies can block a garden bed normally bathed in sunlight when on the ground.

It's easy to understand. You know that the sun rises in the east and sets in the west. When it's midday, the sun is always in the south, and because of this, raised beds facing the south are sunnier and much warmer than the ones placed on the north side of the house. A raised bed is meant to be in direct sunlight for most of the day, so if your backyard is on the north side of the house, but you are fortunate enough to have a lot of space in your front yard, then consider placing your raised bed there. Also, remember that the sun is much higher in summer than it is in winter, so if you plan to extend your planting season, check to see if your garden still gets adequate sunlight even while at its lowest height.

Another way to let more sunlight into your garden is by cutting back overgrown and overhanging vegetation branches. Don't forget to ask your neighbors if they will be okay with reducing the height of a few trees in their garden that affect the amount of sunlight coming into yours. Reducing the height of your boundary fence will also let more light in, even though it might cost you your privacy.

Location

There are also other practical issues to consider when picking a location for your raised bed. If you intend to cultivate herbs or vegetables, then consider placing the raised bed near the back door or kitchen window so you can harvest fresh veggies or herbs easily when cooking. To create more privacy from outsiders, you can consider placing your raised beds on the garden walls to increase the height of your garden boundaries. You can also place them around a seating area or patio to create a sense of privacy. If the plan is to cultivate trees or tall plants, keeping them away from the house is best, so it doesn't restrict your view of the garden.

Provision of Shelter

Just like us, crops often prefer to be protected from the elements. Wind exposure can cause their leaves to decimate. It can also cause the affected crops to dry out quickly as it absorbs most of the moisture in the soil. Strong winds during blossoming periods do not allow pollinating insects to fly around and do their jobs, which will lead to low yields in fruit bushes and trees.

One effective solution is to cultivate tenacious, tough crops capable of tolerating the wind. Plants that thrive in waterfront locations are ideal. However, if your plants are tender, like most vegetables, they will require some protection from strong winds. Many small gardens, especially in town, usually have proper shelter from winds because walls, fences, and hedges surround them. For large gardens, avoid constructing raised beds in conditions that will leave them exposed—atop a hill, for instance.

The perfect windbreak for any garden is a hedge because it lessens the impact of the wind while being semipermeable, allowing adequate air circulation. This is vital because it aids in the prevention of diseases, especially fungus, and the buildup of pests which flourish in still, stagnant conditions. Structures that are non-permeable, like fences and walls, effectively prevent wind damage, but they come with a detrimental catch. Sometimes, the wind may move along the top edge of the fence or wall and take a nosedive right onto the raised bed with more force.

Frost Pockets

So many plants will pay the price if your raised bed is placed in a frost pocket. Frost typically gathers at the lowest parts of the garden because when cold air passes through it, any warm air that arises is replaced. This effect can be worsened if the cold air is not allowed to circulate, and this is usually caused by a permanent solid structure such as a fence or wall at the lowest end of a garden. Seedlings take the brunt of the cold, getting zapped quickly by the frost, while blossoms or young tender shoots will simply wither and die. It also lessens the length of the growing season because the bed will be too cold to grow anything until well into spring.

Keeping your raised bed away from frosty sites will permit early spring cultivation and lengthen the growing season well into autumn. If a frost pocket is unavoidable, prepare to shield the plants and cultivate later in the season to prevent the disappointment that comes with losing your crops to the harsh cold.

Chapter Five: Constructing Your Garden Beds

Simple Steps to Construct a Wooden Raised Bed

1. After picking a location for your raised bed, determine if the native soil is of high quality. If it is, it should be dug out and reserved to fill the bed later.

2. Use a string or rope to outline the perimeter of the bed on the ground.

3. Retaining stakes of a minimum 2 x 2 inch are required for raised beds. These stakes go into the corners of the bed. Place stakes at every 5 feet along the sides for support. Now push them 12 inches deep into the ground.

4. Use galvanized screws to attach the stakes to the retaining wooden boards.

5. Pour the reserved soil or purchased soil into the bed, filling only the lower section. If the grass was removed from the raised bed site, you can place it upside down at the bottom of the bed because it will slowly rot as the season goes by.

6. Now fill the rest of the bed with an equal mix of garden compost and topsoil.

Simple Steps to Construct a Brick Raised Bed

Brick raised beds are more difficult to construct than wooden ones, needing extra practical skills like bricklaying. Don't fret; it's nothing you can't learn. Brick raised beds are unsurprisingly durable once built properly, providing a sturdy, strong bed that is stylish in most locations–backyard, front yard, or garden.

Cutting a Brick

1. Use the edge of a trowel to make a slight groove in the center of the brick.

2. Place a brick bolster in the groove and use a hammer to bang down swiftly to cut the brick clean in half. Don't forget to wear protective eyewear when cutting bricks.

Steps to Construct a Brick Raised Bed

1. Using a string or rope, map out the perimeter of the raised bed.

2. Now build a footing made of concrete to prevent the bed from sinking into the ground. Now make a trench with a depth of 20 inches and width of two bricks. Mix 2 ½ parts sand, 1 part cement, and 3 ½ parts gravel to make the concrete foundation, then use it to line the bottom to a depth of 6 inches. Now, wait for it to dry.

3. Mix 3 parts sand and 1 part cement. Add as much water as needed for an easy-to-use consistency that is flexible enough to coat the entire brickwork, but not too sloppy. The plasticizer helps to keep the cement mixture flexible.

4. The courses of bricks should be laid two bricks wide. Every brick must be laid onto a bed of cement that is only an inch thick. The second layer should be started with half a brick for it to be

staggered with the courses below it. This will reinforce its strength and durability.

5. The first three layers should be high enough to reach the ground level. Now, keep stacking bricks until you reach your preferred height.

6. If you have any chamfered bricks lying around, cement them at the top edge of the bed for protection from dampness and for aesthetics.

7. The inside of the walls should be lined with a permeable material.

8. Pour in compost and topsoil.

Steps to Construct a Herringbone Brick Path

1. To make sure the path is level with the surface, dig out the soil at the location of the path to a depth of an extra inch than the bricks you will be using.

2. Now layer the bottom of the path with sand to a thickness of 1 inch.

3. Place the bricks in a herringbone pattern along the length of your path.

4. Bed the bricks into the layer of sand and then fill any gaps with extra sand.

Garden Paths

If you intend to have multiple raised beds, you need to carefully consider the paths between and around them. Paths create the structure and backbone of any garden design and are important in ensuring that the essential elements of the garden are accessible.

Garden paths need to be practical and functional, but should also look beautiful and complement the existing style of your garden and raised bed. For instance, a rustic wood chip path will beautifully complement a formal brick raised bed.

The Perfect Width

If you hope to walk comfortably between your raised beds, the least width for your path should be 16 inches. If you intend to use a wheelbarrow while gardening, the path should be at least 26 inches in width. If you want it wide enough for wheelchair access, the path should be about 3 to 4 feet wide. Remember that there will be no extra room for anyone else besides the one wheelchair. For extra room, make it 5 feet wide.

Types of Garden Paths

Paving slab or brick path: The sturdiest paths are built with paving slabs or bricks which provide a strong base for your wheelbarrow to move along. If you are going for a rustic look, consider laying them into the soil, pushing them down to the depth of the slab or brick so they are level with the ground. You can also lay them on the sand and simply secure them with a brush of dry cement and sand mixture, watering it after to set it. They are available in a variety of sizes and prices to fit most people's budgets.

If you are not concerned about style, check the dumpsters in your area because people are often getting rid of old paving slabs and bricks. Don't forget to check with the builder or owner before going through their dumpster.

Grass path: This is the most affordable kind of path but requires the most maintenance as it will need to be mowed at least once a week in the growing season. If you choose to lay the grass right up to the sides of the raised bed, the edges also require regular trimming. Some raised beds might cast shade over a good portion of the grass paths. If so, shade-tolerant grass seed is the best option to ensure the grass is green all year long.

Woodchip mulch path: This option is relatively cheap. To construct one, place gravel boards on either side of the path and hold them in place with wooden pegs. Gravel boards are usually 6 to 8 feet long, 3 to 4 inches wide, and 6 inches high. They work to retain the woodchip mulch on the path and keep it from spreading onto other flower beds and lawns.

Now, place a layer of ground-suppressing membrane on the path, and hold them down with metal tent pegs. Finally, the path should be coated with a 2-inch layer of woodchip mulch and raked to level. The wood chip mulch will need to be topped off regularly as it rots or washes away.

Gravel path: The construction of this path is relatively straightforward and cheap. One con is that spilled soil or compost is hard to pack and tidy away. To construct, dig out a base about 6 inches deep. Place treated lumber at the edges to prevent gravel from spreading to unwanted areas. Wooden pegs should be driven in at 3-foot intervals to keep the lumber in place.

Use a roller or a Wacker plate to compact the ground or simply tread it flat if it covers only a small area. A layer of hardcore should be placed at the base of the path, then layered with sand and topped off with a layer of gravel 2 inches thick. Level it with a rake, and you're done.

Common Mistakes to Avoid in Raised Bed Gardening

Poor arrangement: Siting your garden in the wrong area is a big mistake and almost impossible to fix when using a raised bed. The box is usually hard to rearrange or move once you have filled it with soil, installed the water system, and planted your crops.

To avoid this, the first thing to consider when picking a location for your raised bed is the sun. If the orientation is east-west rather than north-south, your plants are less likely to receive the required sunlight for their development. Vegetables need at least six hours of sunlight every day.

Planting shade-loving plants in the sun or vice versa is another issue that most beginners face. For instance, tomatoes require six or more hours of direct sunlight every day. Chiles, eggplants, and other herbs will be happiest in the sunniest part of the raised bed, while peas or lettuce will prefer shady placements.

That said, plants placed on the south side will get the most sunlight, but ensure that they are short enough plants so they do not restrict sunlight from the other crops.

Unsuitable construction materials: Most raised beds are constructed with wood, but they can be built with a variety of other materials. Confirm the materials are safe for use near your crops, particularly edible crops. Safety standards and health regulations usually vary depending on the region or state.

Toxic materials like pressure-treated wood or chemical-treated lumber should be avoided when sourcing for materials to construct your raised bed. Creosote or other harmful chemicals might be contained in older materials, so avoid those too.

Search for sustainable and locally sourced options that haven't been treated, are resistant to rot and long-lasting, and FSC-approved (Forest Stewardship Council). This will ensure that your raised bed stays functional and wonderful for a long time.

Picking the appropriate size: Try not to go with a raised bed bigger than you need. Your beds should be just the right size for easy access and convenience. The recommended size for a typical raised bed is not over 4 feet wide, to enable the gardener to reach the crops in the middle.

If you site your bed close to a fence, it will benefit you to reduce the width to below 30 inches. Also, ensure that you leave enough space between raised beds, at least 2 to 3 feet. Every gardener should be able to walk through pathways and between beds comfortably.

Watering: Watering your plants too much is another common mistake as your plants can drown and rot. Watering them too little is also problematic. Suppose you are unsure of the amount of water required by your raised bed; no need for any guesswork because you can invest in an irrigation system with a smart controller. It has moisture sensors that automatically detect and adjust the amount of water in your garden.

Your irrigation system need not be state of the art or expensive to function properly and save you a lot of time. However, if an irrigation system is out of your budget your crops need not suffer. All you must do is closely observe the soil. Once it appears hard, it's watering time. If you cannot tell by looking at it, grab a handful of soil and squeeze it into a loose ball. If it sticks together, the soil is moisturized enough. Certain plants act as moisture indicators. A good example is lettuce, which quickly wilts when dehydrated. Consider planting indicator plants to help you properly check the moisture content at a glance.

If you don't have an irrigation plan in place when constructing your raised bed, you will have to water the old-fashioned way, with a long hose or watering can. Another option in the absence of an irrigation system is to place a rainwater barrel close to your raised bed for convenience's sake.

Poor soil quality: Just like a living organism, the soil goes through changes and evolutions. Its conditions are affected by rainfall, drainage issues, or runoff. Certain plants feed off the soil more intensely than others. It is vital to pay attention to the kind of soil you use for your garden–it's mineral levels, pH, and the necessary organic matter required to give it a boost.

The kind of soil you put into your raised bed is an important aspect of your crops' future happiness. Avoid using normal potting soil for your garden because it drains rapidly. There are available raised bed soils on the market that are more effective.

You can purchase a DIY testing kit from a hardware store in your area to test your soil annually. This kit helps you discover the kind of soil you need, considering the crops you want to grow. Test your soil before cultivating and throughout the lifetime of your raised bed. To obtain the most effective soil, mix it with equal parts of organic compost. Your plants will surely take advantage of this nutritious addition.

Chemicals: Making use of the wrong chemicals directly on or near your raised beds can severely affect the productivity of your crops. You may think that it is safe to use these chemicals in your garden but away from raised beds, right? Wrong. The wind can carry all that toxicity to your beds, harming your plants.

Chemicals containing herbicides can linger in the dirt for many years, poisoning the soil. Sure, it is important to get rid of the weeds and grass, but if you get too close, you will lose your plants. These chemicals become extra dangerous in the rainy season because runoff water can transport them to other areas of your garden.

Moral of the story: Stay away from toxic herbicides. Instead, mix equal parts of vinegar and hot water to get rid of the weeds and grass. Simply spray the offending plants with the mixture once a day every day until the weeds wilt and turn brown, then uproot the rest by hand.

Your garden pathways will probably also grow grass and weeds eventually, but instead of spraying them or mowing them, which are also good ideas, you can simply build a barrier. Flatten as many cardboard boxes as you need and layer a little mulch on top of your barrier. It is an easy and more durable solution than other options.

Lack of preparation: Proper preparation of the beds between growing seasons will ensure healthy and bountiful harvests. If you fail to prepare your soil for the next season, the crops you grow may be diseased, stunted, or not grow at all.

Rather than plant the same crops in the same position every year, you can cultivate healthier crops by practicing crop rotation and avoiding planting crops of the same family in the same spot or near each other year after year. Fungal diseases, soil infertility, and common pests are issues faced by different plants; to prevent a problem from spilling over to other plants, alternate the positions of your crops every year.

Wrong vegetable choices: Picking suitable vegetables but in the wrong combination is an error that can be corrected later, but choosing the wrong varieties? Your planting season might be more difficult than you hoped. Let's assume you start with a tougher vegetable like asparagus. If you're a beginner, you might become discouraged by the long wait of two or three years for it to produce a harvest. Another mistake beginners make is cultivating a cool-weather crop like cabbage in the wrong season.

To avoid this, begin with the vegetables that are simpler to grow while you figure out the crops that work well for your gardens, like basil, bell peppers, tomatoes, and zucchini.

Ensure that the vegetable options you select are not just easy to cultivate but will also be suitable for yourself and your family. It is pointless to grow lettuce if there are any allergies in your home. Select the vegetables that will be consumed the most, and you will be more likely to be interested in the variety held by your garden.

It is also vital that the options you pick thrive in your yard, because some might not. Certain vegetables are more prone to pests, don't thrive in humid environments, or cannot withstand sudden changes in temperature throughout the year. Always consider the weather of your location.

To start your first year cultivating an all-herb garden with herbs easy to grow both outdoors and in, here's a list of the simplest herbs to start with:

1. Thyme

2. Parsley

3. Basil

4. Mint

5. Cilantro

6. Oregano

Not using row/seed indicators: Mark your rows and mark the spots where you plant every new addition to your raised bed to prevent overcrowding. It is easy to lose track of the exact spots you put seeds in, but using an indicator will prevent you from replanting over seeds because seedlings can sometimes be mistaken for weeds.

For convenience's sake, place a label where every plant is. Purchase small plastic tags and stick them in the soil to label the plants.

Gardening is an adventure where you never stop learning. Even the most experienced gardeners make mistakes now and then, but learning from these errors is the only way forward. Plus, there's no harm in trying out something new!

Chapter Six: Choosing Cultivars (Plus Tips for Organic Gardening)

This chapter will guide beginners in the field through the sometimes-frustrating process of seed selection and garden preparation. It is also for experienced gardeners who may be dealing with seed-shopping addiction.

The first thing to do is understand the jargon because, like other trades, seed catalogs have certain phrases and terminologies that are crucial to understand. You may know the meaning of the certified organic label (and it is okay to be unaware. This label ensures that these seeds have been cultivated in organic soil and have been cared for and processed according to the guidelines issued by the USDA). However, the description of seeds goes a little further than that. Here are a few important terminologies you will discover in the catalogs:

1. Cool-season plants: These are plant species tolerant of the frost. They thrive in fall and spring when temperatures in the daytime are in the 70s or 60s, and nighttime temperatures range from 30 to 40 degrees.

2. Warm-season plants: These flourish from late spring well into early fall when the temperature in the daytime is over 80 degrees, and nighttime temperatures are typically over 50 degrees.

3. Days to full growth: This is the average number of days required for transplanted crops started indoors to reach maturity. It is also the number of days required for seeds sown directly in the garden to mature.

4. Disease resistant: These two words are the most crucial to look out for when going through seed catalog listings. Some listings contain acronyms like VFNTSt or VFN, which is a shorthand tag for the particular disease that a variety is immune to. A VFN berry is immune to fusarium wilt, nematodes, and verticillium wilt. Every seed catalog should come with a cipher for its disease-resistant codes.

5. Heirloom: These are traditional varieties that have been passed down through generations, instead of being produced by modern seed farmers. The majority of the heirlooms available today predate the 1940s.

6. Open-pollinated: These varieties have been naturally pollinated by insects or the wind, instead of the controlled pollination methods used by experienced breeders. A seed from an open-pollinated plant can be reserved yearly because it will germinate true from seed, that is, it will look almost identical to its parent plant.

7. F1 hybrid: These seeds are a product of a deliberate crossing of two varieties. F1 hybrids give rise to plants with greater consistency in appearance, size, and other characteristics. The seed produced cannot be reserved and planted the next season again because it will grow into plants that have significantly different traits than the original plant.

8. Non-GMO: This seed is not created using any genetic engineering methods. Examples are heirlooms, F1 hybrids, open-pollinated seeds, and any variety bearing a certified organic label. Most of the retail seed companies sell their products as non-GMO, but honestly, there are no GMO seeds available for sale to home

gardeners. Non-GMO seeds are almost strictly used in North America for industrial agriculture.

9. Pelleted variety: These are seeds that have been layered with a biodegradable substance to increase its size and make it easier to cultivate. It helps to lessen the overplanting of small seeds, like carrots and lettuce.

Additionally, be on the lookout for phrases or terminologies that might point out a trait you think will be useful to you. For instance, a "bush type" bean is a kind of bean that grows stocky and low, which makes it a perfect choice for gardens with limited space. There are also "patio tomatoes," which grow stocky and short, and have been bred to flourish in a container or pot. Speak to your neighbors or friends about the varieties they prefer or contact your local cooperative extension service officer for suggestions on what seeds to plant.

The Link Between Climate and Vegetables

It is okay to select some seed varieties that will require more time and attention than others because they aren't designed to thrive in your climate. It is recommended, though, to purchase seed varieties that have no complaints about the climate in your region.

The first thing to focus on is discovering your first gardening window. This is the approximate number of days in a year free of frost. This is important because the growth of many crops comes to a halt when the temperature plummets below 32° F. To do this, mark the day the frost ends in spring and the day of the first frost in fall in your area.

Some vegetables like basil, melon, tomatoes, beans, corn, cucumbers, and so on are warm-seasonal. They are unlikely to survive the first frost of the year, so they must be cultivated and harvested during the gardening window. Other vegetables like cabbages, potatoes, carrots, and so on are cold-seasonal. They are more likely to survive a mild frost. However, they rarely make it through the summer unless they are in the north or coastal regions where the summers are cooler. If you live in an area with hot summers, only cultivate these kinds of crops in fall and spring.

When you purchase a seed packet, check for an indicator that reveals the 'days to full growth' of that seed variety. You are unlikely to find that information in the catalog listings as they only tell you the regions suited to the crops. Crops that require 90 days or more to maturity are unlikely to survive in areas with short, cool summers because they are heat lovers. The number of days to full growth written on the seed packet will simply show you the intensity of warmth or coolness needed by the crop to thrive, not necessarily indicate the exact number of days required by the seed to mature.

Tips for Organic Gardening

Cultivating organic edible plants means you and your family can enjoy tasty, fresh, and healthy harvests free of pesticides or synthetic chemicals. Some of the basic tips for organic gardening are the same as in nonorganic gardening: Place your plants in an area that gets maximum sunlight for about 6 hours a day or more. All gardens need to be regularly watered, so ensure that you have a hose or spigot that will reach all parts of your bed. Now, we will look at the tips particular to only organic gardening.

Begin with mulch and organic garden soil: To enjoy the harvests of a healthy organic garden, you must begin with healthy soil. The most vital part of a soil's makeup is the organic matter such as compost, manure, or peat moss, which is a product of decayed microorganisms of former plant life. This decayed matter supplies the crops with the necessary nutrients for their survival. It is possible to create your own compost by setting aside a bin or area where the organic matter will be left to decay. Or you can just purchase it in bulk if you own a lot of raised beds. You can also use bagged compost, available at home improvement stores or garden centers.

Limit the spread of weeds by layering a 2-inch thick coat of mulch on the soil. It forms a barrier that keeps weed from receiving the sunlight they need to germinate. This layer of mulch also prevents spores of fungal disease from drifting onto plant leaves. Use an organic material like weed-free straw, newspaper, or cocoa hulls as mulch so it will decompose, contributing to the organic matter in the soil.

Don't ever settle for inorganic garden fertilizer: Using fertilizer in your garden will ensure that your crops grow faster and produce larger crops. The types of organic fertilizer you should look for are well-decayed manure from plant-eating critters like horses, chickens, sheep, etc., pre-packaged organic fertilizer purchased at your neighborhood garden store or online. A variety of organic fertilizers can also be found at home improvement stores and garden centers. Note that if your soil is already rich in nutrients, you can consider skipping fertilizer. Too much goodness can attract pests as they will be drawn to the lush growth of your crops.

Tips for seedling shopping: When you shop for seedlings, you should choose plants that have no yellow leaves and a healthy color for the species. Steer clear of wilting or droopy leaves. If you're in the market for transplants, carefully tap the plant out of the container or pot to ensure that the roots are white and well developed. Stay away from plants that already have flowers or are budding. If they can't be avoided, pinch the flowers and buds off before planting to make sure the plant directs its energy into forming new roots.

Rotate your crops every year: A lot of closely related plants usually suffer the same disease, so it is necessary to avoid growing crops in the same spot where their relatives grew a year or two prior. The two biggest plant families to look out for are the squash family, like pumpkin, watermelon, squash, and so on, and the tomato family like potatoes, tomatoes, peppers, eggplant, and so on. Crop rotation to various parts of the garden will help limit or prevent disease development and depletion of the soil's nutrients.

Dealing with weeds: Those pesky plants that seem to sprout from nowhere overnight are every gardener's pet peeve. Plan to weed your raised beds daily. Uprooting weeds is easier to do after watering or rainfall, but if the soil is muddy or wet, postpone the weeding until it dries out a little.

There are various ways to uproot a weed. One way is to gently pinch the base of the stem and tug out the root. Another way is levering out the root system using a weeding trowel. A hoe can also scrape off the top of the weed, taking care not to harm any crops. Remember that weeds will grow back if their roots are left in the soil.

Weeds are bad for your garden for many valid reasons. They not only compete with your crops for nutrients and water, but they also attract pests. If pests eventually find their way into your raised bed, they move from one plant to another, spreading disease. The best and most organic way to get rid of them is to pick them off by hand. If you hate insects or are squeamish, gloves might make you feel more comfortable.

Your garden should always be clean: Many diseases are spread rapidly through fallen, dead foliage. So inspect your raised bed at least once a week, or more if you can, to clean up shed leaves. It is possible to prevent a whole disease outbreak simply by getting rid of one infected leaf. Dispose of the diseased or dead leaves in a bin, never your compost pile.

Ensure that your plants are getting enough water and air: Watering your leaves in the afternoon or evening can promote the growth of mildews like downy or powdery mildew. Rather than water your crops from above, invest in a water-saving soaker hose that will deliver water straight to the roots, preventing splashing. Also, adhere to the spacing requirements on the seed packets to prevent crowding. Adequate airflow between crops can help prevent an outbreak of many fungal diseases.

Grow plants that attract beneficial insects: There are certain flowers that not only add beauty to your garden but also attract helpful insects like bumblebees that help with pollination and praying mantis and lady beetles that help devour harmful insects. Some of these flowers include:

1. Cleome

2. Daisy

3. Bachelor's button

4. Marigold

5. Purple coneflower

6. Cosmos

7. Nasturtium

8. Black-eyed Susan

9. Zinnia

10. Sunflower

11. Salvia

12. Yarrow

Chapter Seven: Vegetables for Raised Beds

When preparing for your raised bed garden, it is so easy to get overwhelmed by the many different plants in the seed catalogs. However, there are helpful tips to assist you in finding the right crops to grow.

Picking which plants to cultivate in your garden can be loads of fun, especially for beginners just itching to try everything. Looking through seed catalogs and marking out the seeds you are interested in cultivating is an exciting experience because the possibilities are endless. It is quite common to see beginner gardeners going overboard planting more crops than they need. Planning before planting is the smart route to take in order not to overwhelm yourself when all the harvests are ready at the same time.

How to Select Crops for Your Raised Bed Garden

This is time to think about what you intend to achieve with the garden. What, exactly, is the plan?

Do you aim to supplement your meals with fresh, organic produce?

Are you hoping to redirect the money you'd usually spend on groceries to something else?

Are you trying to avoid pesticides?

Do you plan to cultivate foods that can be preserved and stored through winter?

Chances are that the aim of planting your edible garden includes one or more of the points I will mention in this chapter. Having a clear picture of your objectives will help you better select the right crops that will be the most productive in your growing space. Here is a list of certain considerations when choosing crops for your raised bed garden:

Go for crops you and your family like eating: Unless you are an industrial gardener, it is pointless to put effort into tending to crops you or your family don't even like. Select crops based on your food preferences and that of your family. Gardening is especially satisfying when you are rewarded with the foods you like to eat.

If you enjoy salads, then greens, cabbages, lettuce, and tomatoes are great choices for your raised beds. If you like to have fresh salsa now and then, then onions, cilantro, peppers, and tomatoes should make the list. If you're not sure of the foods you enjoy, think for a minute about the foods you pick up often when you visit the farmer's market or produce section of the grocery store. What goes into the cart week after week? Yes, your garden might be small, but you will save a few bucks when you grow your own food.

Choose crops that thrive in your region: As mentioned earlier, seek information about the growing season and climate of your region. The best way to obtain this information is by speaking to other gardeners in the area. Suppose you have a gardener for a neighbor–even better. Talk to them about the crops they grow in their garden and the issues they face. Gardeners are naturally generous with their experiences and successful gardening tips.

High-value crops should make the list as well: What kind of vegetables do you enjoy eating but buy in little quantities and only when there is a sale? Do you see where I'm going with this? Growing crops that are usually expensive makes sense.

Common high-value crops are heirloom tomatoes, garlic, salad greens, and sweet bell peppers. For instance, a pack of organic lettuce goes for about $5 at the grocery store. But a pack of high-quality lettuce seeds go for less and will produce over six pounds of organic lettuce. Another class of high-value crops is herbs. During the growing season, cultivating an abundance of herbs to spice up your meals and preserve for winter is a good idea.

Consider replacing produce that has been contaminated with pesticide residue: The produce from some farms that is found in grocery stores has been contaminated with pesticide residue, whether consumers know this or not. Cultivating your own crops will guarantee you fresh organic produce, free of pesticides and other chemicals. This way, you get to eradicate completely or heavily reduce your intake of toxins.

A dirty dozen list is issued by the Environmental Working Group every year. This list contains the top twelve farm produce items that have tested positive for pesticide loads by the USDA. Crops that made the list this year include:

1. Spinach
2. Nectarines
3. Peaches
4. Strawberries
5. Cherries
6. Kale
7. Pears

8. Potatoes

9. Tomatoes

10. Celery

11. Apples

12. Grapes

These crops and more are easy to cultivate in your raised bed garden with zero chemicals.

Select crops that are easy to cultivate: If you are a beginner in the field or don't have enough time on your hands to tend to crops constantly, then consider cultivating crops that do not need to be coddled. One of the main reasons people give up on their gardening interests out of frustration is because they simply have no time for watering and weeding, which can be a lot of work. Certain crops don't require a lot of attention and care. Crops like artichokes, walking onions, asparagus, and many more.

Consider crops for preserving: If your goal is to preserve your harvest, you will have to plant enough to eat and to store. This can take a few seasons of experimenting to find your balance. Keep records of your experience and progress and adjust the number of crops every year.

There will be that time of year when your kitchen counter will be piled with tomatoes waiting to be transformed into salsas and tomato sauce. You will have carrots and string beans liking your refrigerator's crisper drawers eager to be pressure canned, and cucumbers ready to be turned into pickles. It can be overwhelming sometimes, but the end goal is always worth it. Therefore, it is important to consider yours and your family's nutritional needs first before selecting crops to plant. Also, think of the quantity of food consumed on average.

Note that certain vegetables like peppers, summer squashes, eggplants, and tomatoes grow and produce harvest throughout the growing season. Then there are others that only produce once, like carrots, garlic, onions, and radishes. Once you are done selecting the crops that you'd like in your raised beds, the next things to do are get organized, make lists, buy seeds, and get planting! Good planning is such an underrated aspect of gardening and is the key to a bountiful harvest. It doesn't matter if you are a beginner or have been gardening for years. You will benefit from planning every year.

Easy Vegetables to Plant in Your Raised Bed Garden

Many vegetables will thrive in a raised bed garden, but this is a list of the ones absolutely in love with the structured space provided by a raised bed.

1. Kale: This is one of the best greens to grow in a raised bed because it continues to produce well into the cool autumn season. With a raised bed, it is easy to cover the hardy kale with cold frames that will extend its productive season. You can use old box-framed windows to do this. If you live in a region with mild or short winters, you can ensure that your kales grow strong in winter with these raised beds.

2. Swiss chard: This vegetable revels in the supportive atmosphere created by the raised bed. They enjoy the loose soil and dense nutrients that ensure a lot of growth and tender, bright stalks. Grow this vegetable with kale and keep them producing well into the winter.

3. Carrots: So many gardeners suffer from terrible carrot harvest because they turn out stunted if grown in quickly packed-down soil; raised beds give them the perfectly loose soil they need to thrive. Long carrots require tall, deep beds while tiny French carrots prefer short, low beds. Raised beds produce large and healthy carrots without all the stunted roots and knobs that conventional beds usually produce.

4. Parsnips: Like carrots, parsnips require soil packed with nutrients but loose enough to allow them to grow strong. These sweet roots will be grateful to be among the vegetables in your raised bed.

5. Tomatoes: Tomatoes are heavy feeders that germinate and spread to as many areas as they can. They are the perfect raised bed crop. They despise weeds and require a lot of attention and care to protect them from slugs and other insects. Construct a raised bed with four posters and use some twine to fence it in. This will provide space for your tomatoes to thrive.

6. Cucumbers: Cucumbers grow especially well in raised beds because they need soil with good drainage. When planted in the right conditions, it is safe to expect the crunchy, fresh, and tender cucumbers that are almost a dream to some. However, the cucumbers will harden if the soil stagnates. Their vines tend to take over the entire bed, so it is advised to place them in a separate bed and build them something to climb on.

7. Leeks: All onions thrive in raised beds because they are provided with well-drained soil and plenty of nitrogen, but leeks have taken a special liking to this method of gardening. Construct a low but long raised bed and grow your leeks as a stylish border in your garden. They don't take up as much space as tomatoes or cucumbers. They create a beautiful visual divider, giving you a full harvest of thick, tall leeks for autumn stews and soups.

8. Zucchinis: Every gardener knows that zucchini can sometimes be very overwhelming. It takes up the entire garden, producing more zucchinis than farmers need. Placing it in a raised bed will do nothing to reduce its yield, but it will prevent it from taking up all the space in your garden. Its spreading stems and wide leaves will be given their own space. Don't attempt to plant anything else in the same raised bed as your zucchinis, with horseradish being the only exception.

9. Lettuce: Head lettuces make a beautiful addition to a raised bed garden. They are beautiful balls of dark green, bright green, or red-tipped green goodness. They also enjoy the warm loose soil and fewer weeds that come with raised beds. They can also be planted early in the season and keep producing until later in the season.

10. Beets: These roots are quite easy to grow. They love the loamy soil, but that isn't a problem for raised bed gardeners because literally, any soil can be purchased and piled into a raised bed. They can be planted all alone or share space with horseradish, another root crop that also enjoys pampering, fewer weeds, and friable soil. With raised beds, you can provide an environment perfectly designed for the beets, soil that is properly drained and contains the right amount of nitrogen. They also keep the horseradish in check, preventing them from spreading to other parts of the garden.

11. Salad vegetables: Cultivating salad greens like spinach and arugula in a raised bed is great, especially if you own dogs or chickens. Raised beds keep these greens inaccessible to intrusive pets, and the borders keep them well guarded against digging and scratching. Like lettuces, fragile salad greens also enjoy the warm soil and great drainage associated with raised beds.

12. Melons: This is another plant that will attempt to take over your garden! Place your melons in trellises in taller raised beds to contain them and protect them from slugs while they grow. Melons are slow-ripening crops, so they require a well-drained and more controlled environment or they are likely to rot on the damp earth. Cultivating melons in raised beds also gives you the chance to pay attention to the soil. The soil required to grow melons need to be consistently kept warm, and the raised bed environment is easier to manipulate than ground beds. Put your melons in raised beds over 6 feet high, and ensure that the soil is packed with organic matter.

13. Radishes: Radishes are assumed to be easy to grow, but the truth is that radishes are picky, moody little roots. They hate soggy conditions, dry conditions, over-rich soil, clay soil, and hot weather. They are the princesses of the plant world and will enjoy the lavish, controlled environment of a raised bed. Construct the perfect raised bed for your choosy radishes, throw in the perfect soil, and ensure it is well-drained but not dry. Do this, and you will be able to brag to everyone about the ease of growing radishes.

14. Potatoes: Mix your raised bed soil with lots of straw, and you will be pleasantly surprised at the ease with which your rootlets will grow into huge potatoes. These tubers are completely in love with everything about raised beds, which some people might find unexpected. Besides, potatoes are easier to harvest from raised beds because all you have to do is sit beside your bed and gently pull on the roots, instead of bending all the time.

15. Broccoli Raab: Broccoli can grow wherever space is provided for it, but broccoli raab is much smaller than the regular broccoli, so it easy for it to get overwhelmed by larger crops and lose water and nutrients when sharing space. Give your rapini its own home with an old wooden trunk. This tasty vegetable can be planted early in the season when the soil is warm, and because it grows rapidly, you can harvest multiple times before the season is over.

16. Celery: This is another picky crop that is practically demanding when grown in a raised bed. It requires rich, constantly damp soil and a long productive season. Your celery will show its appreciation for your attention by becoming more tender and tastier than you ever hoped.

17. Bok choy: A fast-growing, intense feeder, bok choy requires loose, rich soil. It doesn't appreciate sharing its space with weeds, which make it perfect for raised beds, especially in northern regions. It is a cool-weather crop that can keep growing well into the late fall, even without a lot of protection from the cold.

Chapter Eight: The Best Trees for Raised Beds

Small trees on decks or patios can add privacy, style, provide shade, act as natural focal points, and even produce fruit. The good thing is that a lot of these trees can grow well in raised beds or containers. Some possess special features like vivid fall colors, flowers, and attractive bark. However, some trees have messy features like dropping flowers, seeds, fruits, and others, and not everyone is comfortable with that. So, you must know all the features of the tree you intend to plant, and its survivability in your region.

Small Trees for Your Raised Bed

Here is a list of 13 amazing small trees to cultivate in your raised bed. Note: To select the perfect tree for your space, you need to consider its height and width at maturity. Also, some roots tend to crack or lift pavement, which would make it unsuited for a patio. If you plan to cultivate your tree in a pot, remember to check on it regularly to know when the roots need a new pot due to expansion.

Chaste Tree: This tree is an Asian and Mediterranean native with a lot of trunks that can be conditioned to create a nice shade tree. Its leaves are extraordinarily aromatic, producing tiny fragrant flowers on spikes during the fall and summer. The varieties latifolia and roses produce pink flowers, while silver spire and alba produce white blossoms, and it can be transformed into a shrub through pruning. Prune this tree every late winter to maintain its shape. The chaste tree is highly resistant to oak root fungus and is also heat-resistant.

Colors available: White, Pink, Lavender-blue.

Soil Requirements: Well-drained, loose soil, medium moisture.

Sun Exposure: Maximum sunlight.

Kumquat: Also called Citrus japonica, this tree can be cultivated in pots or on the ground. If they are planted on the ground, they can grow as big as 8 feet tall and 6 feet wide. The container versions are not as big but still as beautiful. Their bright orange flowers eventually transform into tangy edible fruit, and dark green leaves are a sight for sore eyes.

Plant kumquats in your raised bed for their bright orange fruits and aromatic blooms. They are a great addition to any garden, but they must be taken indoors during cold winters. Kumquats need to be relocated to a larger raised bed or container every two or three years and fertilized throughout the growing season.

Colors available: White.

Soil requirements: Wet clay or sandy loam.

Sun exposure: Maximum sunlight.

Japanese Maple: This tree is also called Acer palmatum. It is a naturally huge tree, growing up to 15 feet high at maturity. It can be cultivated on the ground and in raised beds. In raised beds, be prepared to transplant the tree to another bed every year due to a yearly increase in size.

There are different varieties of the Japanese maple, but the best ones for raised beds have finely cut, threadlike leaves and weeping branches. They include the Butterfly, Red Dragon, Crimson Queen,

Mikawa Yatsubusa, Burgundy Lace, and Dissectum varieties. Japanese maples need not be pruned often. However, ensure that you rid the tree of damaged, diseased, or dead branches when you spot them.

Colors available: Red-purple.

Soil requirements: Slightly acidic, moist, rich, and well-drained.

Sun exposure: Maximum sunlight to partial shade.

Ficus: This tree is also called Ficus benjamina or weeping fig, and it can grow to a height of at least 50 feet in the wild, but when domesticated, it becomes a houseplant. It is a very eye-catching tree with its twisty, arching branches and bright green leaves.

Ficus makes a flexible patio plant that can transition easily from an indoor to an outdoor tree. It doesn't like the cold but can withstand the outdoors after the spring frost has passed. This tree requires monthly fertilization in the growing season but would prefer to be left alone during winter.

Colors available: Burgundy, green-purple, blue.

Soil Requirements: Well-drained, rich, and moist.

Sun exposure: Maximum sunlight to partial shade.

European Fan Palm: This tree, also called Chamaerops humilis, is perfect if you are looking to give your deck or patio a tropical vibe because the striking silhouette of the tree is an absolute beauty. There are also other species bred for small spaces including the paradise palm (Howea forsteriana), the Chinese fan palm (Livistona chinensis), the pygmy date palm (Phoenix roebelenii), the Lady palm (Rhapis excelsa), and the Windmill palm (Trachycarpus fortune). Always remember to fertilize your palm throughout the growing season and cut off any diseased or dead portions when they are spotted. Also, try not to overwater it because palms don't like that.

Colors available: Yellow.

Soil Requirements: Well-drained, rich, and slightly moist.

Sun exposure: Maximum sunlight to partial shade.

Ornamental Crabapple: This tree is also called a malus or flowering crabapple and is appreciated more for its short but worthy displays of pink, white and red flowers than its edible fruits. You can plant the smallest varieties in pots or containers while the others can be trained against a fence or wall as an espalier.

The varieties bred for large, raised beds are the Indian Magic, Sargent, Centurion, and Japanese, also called M. floribunda. Crabapple trees become more tolerant of the drought as they mature, but ensure that their soil doesn't dry out. If you experience long periods without rainfall, especially in the warmer months, water your tree. Also, they need to be pruned a little, outside the regular maintenance of removing diseased, dead, or damaged branches.

Colors available: White, red, and pink.

Soil Requirements: Well-drained, partly moist, and rich.

Sun exposure: Maximum sunlight.

Ornamental Plum or Cherry: This tree is sometimes called a flowering prunus. They are adorned with dark purple leaves and red, white, or pink flowers based on the variety. They can be planted in raised beds or large containers. A few varieties are susceptible to fungal disease and insect attacks, so ensure that you prune your tree to thin out the branches a little bit, improving air circulation, which helps to prevent these issues.

Small varieties of the flowering plums include Krauter Vesuvius purple leaf plum, also called Prunus cerasifera; Krauter Vesuvius; Double pink flowering plum, also called Prunus x blireana; and the purple leaf plum, also called Prunus cerasifera.

Small varieties of the flowering cherries include Yoshino cherry (Japanese flowering cherry), Okame (Prunus incisa x Prunus campanulata); Purple leaf sand cherry (Prunus x cisterna), and Albertii (Prunus padus).

Colors available: Red, white, and pink.

Soil requirements: Partly moist and well drained.

Sun exposure: Maximum sunlight to partial shade.

Pine: Also called Pinus, these evergreen trees provide you with something green to decorate your patio throughout the year. Plus, they provide a good amount of privacy and shade throughout the year. They like to be pruned frequently, so keep them as petite as you like. Certain species are bred for decks and patios like the Lacebark pine (Pinus bungeana), evergreen Japanese red pine (Pinus densiflora), and the evergreen Swiss stone pine (Pinus cembra).

For large, raised beds or containers, consider growing the Evergreen Japanese black pine (Pinus thunbergiana), and the evergreen mugo pine (Pinus mugo). Pine trees rarely need a lot of care. Simply water them during prolonged droughts and fertilize yearly if you have poor soil.

Colors available: Nonflowering.

Soil Requirements: Well-drained, fertile, and partly moist.

Sun exposure: Maximum sunlight to partial shade.

Smoke Tree: Also called the smoke bush, this tree is popular for its striking dark reddish-purple leaves and hairs so silky they look like puffs of smoke. It can be cultivated in a large container or raised bed, and near a patio or deck. The smoke effect is because of the fluffy hairs that accompany the tree's bloom in spring. The hairs transition from pink to purple as the summer progresses. Ensure that you prune very lightly in early spring to get the best blooms.

Colors available: Yellow.

Soil requirements: Well-drained and partly moist.

Sun exposure: Maximum sunlight.

Ornamental Pear: This tree is also called Pyrus. You will require at least two pear trees to cross-pollinate and produce fruit. If you have space for only one tree, choose between Bartlett or Anjou because they are the varieties with the ability to self-pollinate to an extent. Other small varieties for raised beds include Edgedell pear, Manchurian pear, Jack flowering pear, Snow pear, and Glen's Form. Pear trees have no issues with wet soil if they are provided with appropriate drainage. They are also prone to a disease known as fire blight, so you will need to prune off the diseased potions when they are identified to prevent the spread.

Colors available: White.

Soil requirements: Humus, well-drained, and moist.

Sun exposure: Maximum sunlight to partial shade.

Sweet Bay: This is also called Laurus nobilis. It is a tiny, slender evergreen shaped like a cone. Its leaves are highly aromatic and a dark green color. Its leaves are the exact bay leaves used for cooking many types of meals. It is a good choice for raised beds or containers placed on patios or decks. It can be pruned into a hedge or a topiary. It can tolerate drought but not for long periods, so water it when you experience long periods without rainfall. Yes, it loves to bask in a lot of light; however, shield it from the sun during hot afternoons, especially during warm months.

Colors available: Yellow-green.

Soil Requirements: Well-drained, rich, and moist.

Sun exposure: Maximum sunlight to partial shade.

Crepe Myrtle: Also called shrubs, these trees are extremely popular in the southern parts of the United States for their bright pink blooms, beautiful bark, and gorgeous fall leaves. You can plant the full-size varieties in large raised beds as they will grow as tall as 10 feet or choose from the many smaller varieties like Peppermint Lace, Zuni, Acoma, Hopi, Catawba, Chica Pink, Yuma, Pink Velour, Centennial, Seminole, White Chocolate, Glendora White, Chica Red, and Comanche. Try not to fertilize excessively because this can lead to excessive leaf growth. Excessive pruning is also unnecessary, although you can shape your tree early in spring if you wish.

Colors available: Pink and white.

Soil requirements: Partly moist and well-drained.

Sun exposure: Maximum sunlight.

Wisteria: Besides the obvious beauty of this tree, it can be conditioned as a shrub, small tree, or vine. If you want a tree, cut off all the stems, leaving only one and tying it to a wooden stake. When it has grown to the preferred height, pinch or prune the branch tips to force the growth of more branches. Wisteria can also be planted to layer a pergola or an arbor. The two most popular Wisteria species are Japanese Wisteria, also called W. floribunda, and the Chinese Wisteria, also called Wisteria sinensis. Don't use fertilizer unless your soil isn't rich enough, but feel free to layer a bit of compost to promote healthy growth and blooming.

Colors available: Purple, white, and pink.

Soil Requirements: Rich, moist, and well-drained.

Sun exposure: Maximum sunlight.

Chapter Nine: Raised Bed Herb Garden

People have used herbs for their healing and culinary properties for centuries. Today, herbs remain as useful and even more popular than ever. Chefs adore the unique flavors that herbs bring to all types of food and drink. Herbalists appreciate the healing properties of certain leaves, roots, and flowers. Herbal crafters preserve the fragrance and beauty of flowers and leaves in sachets, potpourri, dried arrangements, and wreaths. And gardeners love herbs for all their outstanding qualities, like their low maintenance, natural resistance to insects, and their vigor.

When many people think of herbs, it is common to picture the basic kitchen seasonings like rosemary, thyme, basil, and sage, but herbs are any plant that is deemed useful. For example, the seeds, flowers, leaves, roots, or stems of an herb can be highly valued for their medicine, dye, flavoring, fragrance, or some other benefit. It doesn't even have to be about function; many gardeners grow herbs simply because of how beautiful they are.

Where to Plant Herbs

Many herbs can survive in typical garden soil, if there is good enough drainage. Certain herbs like rosemary, bay, and lavender are woody plants with origins in the Mediterranean and thrive in sharply drained, gritty soil. Proper drainage is especially important because the roots of plants native to the Mediterranean tend to rot in moist soil. This is one reason why raised beds are perfect for cultivating herbs.

A lot of herbs flourish in full sunlight, enjoying at least six hours of direct sunlight daily. If your garden space doesn't receive as much sun, then consider herbs that don't require as much. Ideal choices include:

1. Parsley
2. Shiso
3. Mint
4. Cilantro
5. Chives
6. Tarragon

Like other crops, herbs can suffer when exposed to windy sites. Cultivating your herbs next to other buildings, walls, or next to your house provides for the warm and protective microclimate needed for them to thrive. It also increases your chances of a successful harvest with fragile perennials like rosemary. It doesn't matter if you grow the rosemary in a container and take it indoors during the winter, it is still recommended to spread it out in a sheltered but sunny area.

Where to Get Herbs for Planting

Certain herbs are fairly easy to begin from seed, but others take longer to germinate. Purchase slow-growing herbs at a nursery or simply divide existing plants if you have any. Some herbs can also be grown from cuttings.

Growing Herbs from Seed

Before planting any herb directly in your raised bed or seed-starting trays, go through the seed packet, which will help you with all the important information. Herbs that can easily be grown from seed include:

1. Borage
2. Chervil
3. Dill
4. Basil
5. Cilantro
6. Parsley
7. Calendula
8. Sage

Growing Herbs from Division

Perennial herbs can be easily divided. To do this, dig up the plant's root system using a garden fork and either use your hands to pull the roots apart or use a knife to cut the roots into as many pieces as you need, then replant them in your raised bed. You can also place a few divisions in pots to develop indoors well into the winter. If you plan to place the divisions outside, the ideal time to do this is fall. Herbs get established more quickly when divided and replanted in autumn. Perennials easily grown from division include:

1. Lovage
2. Oregano
3. Chives
4. Thyme
5. Bee balm
6. Marjoram

7. Garlic chives

Growing Herbs from Cutting

This method of growing herbs should be practiced in the summer or spring when plants are healthy, strong, and growing vigorously. Tarragon and rosemary have sturdy roots in the fall, which makes them great candidates for cuttings. Ideal choices for this method of growing herbs include:

1. Oregano

2. Thyme

3. Lavender

4. Sage

5. Mint

Steps to Grow Herbs from Cuttings

1. Pick stem portions that are tender and fresh, not woody. They also must be at least three inches long, with more than four leaves on them. Find a leaf node facing outwards and slash right above it with your knife.

2. Now pluck the leaves off the lower part of the stem and sprinkle rooting hormone powder all over the cut end.

3. Prepare a four-inch pot, filling it with wet potting soil. Now drive the stem about two inches deep into the pot.

4. Lightly cover the cuttings with a plastic bag because they need to be kept in moist conditions and away from intense sunlight. Avoid watering them until you absolutely must, and remove the covering if the area looks too moisturized.

5. Be on the lookout for fresh leaf sprouts in the first weeks because it means that the cuttings are properly rooted.

6. Time to move the newly sprouted plants into your raised beds filled with normal and healthy planting soil. This time, the raised bed must be placed under direct sunlight.

Growing Herbs in Planters and Pots

There are many advantages of cultivating herbs in planters and pots. They enable you to grow delicate perennials like flowering sages and rosemary throughout the year if you take them indoors during the fall.

1. Always begin with high-quality potting soil. This soil ensures good drainage. Avoid using normal garden soil because they tend not to have good drainage when placed in raised beds. Just like other plants in raised beds, herbs need to be regularly fertilized and watered throughout the growing season. Herbs native to the Mediterranean, like rosemary, have a high tolerance for partly dry soil, but only for short periods. Other herbs require more attention to watering, especially ones with broader leaves. During the growing season, when they are outdoors, use a liquid fertilizer according to the instructions on the package. When you bring them inside during winter, there won't be any need for much fertilization, except once or twice a month. Herbs can thrive in any well-drained, reasonably fertile soil, which makes raised beds or containers ideal for herb gardening.

2. Growing herbs need access to good lighting. If you can construct a hard path with bright-colored, reflecting paving, that would be great. Concrete or pebble panels are used in herb gardens to reflect light onto the growing plants, creating a warm enough environment on chilly nights.

3. Herbs typically require little fertilizer and produce without a lot of feeding. Feeding can reduce the concentration of flavors.

4. A lot of herbs require soil with pH ranging from neutral to alkaline.

5. Intense levels of direct sunlight are crucial for producing good herb flavor, so your herbs should be placed in the most lit area of your garden.

Amazing Raised Bed Herbs

Here are my favorite raised bed herbs:

Basil: Also called Ocimum basilicum, this herb is a major ingredient in many recipes, particularly Mediterranean classics and summer salads. Basil is the most sold herb in all of Britain. Despite having origins in India, where it is regarded as sacred, it flourishes on British soil and is perfect for any raised bed.

How to cultivate: This delicate annual cannot withstand the cold and frost. It can only be cultivated outdoors during summer and must be taken indoors in colder months. It must be grown in fertile soil and be exposed to as much light and warmth as possible. Greenhouses are perfect, same as kitchen windowsills, to keep basil thriving for a long period. There are many available varieties, so experiment with as many as you like this summer and relish the tastes on your pasta dishes and homemade salads.

Chives: Also called Allium schoenoprasum, this hardy perennial is especially easy to cultivate. Chives are a great addition to your herb garden as they are popular for their beautiful purple blossoms. Once upon a time, they were once strung up in bunches to ward off evil spirits, but they are a major kitchen ingredient today. All parts of the plant are edible, which makes it extremely versatile. Its flowers can be used to garnish various salads while the leaves and bulbs can add flavor to many meals. Having a light onion flavor, chives come in handy when preparing all kinds of summer dishes like omelets, classic potato salad, and soups.

How to cultivate: Chives are very low maintenance. You need only to plant them in soil and ensure that they are kept in a sunny spot where they can receive direct sunlight for at least five hours.

Mint: This is also known as common mint, spearmint, or Mentha spicata. It is a hardy herb that can be easily cultivated in any garden. It flowers light purple blossoms throughout August and September. Being a perennial, mint can be trusted to grace your garden year after year. It is vigorous by nature, so don't be surprised if it invades other parts of your garden. To avoid this, plant it in a bottomless raised bed set on the ground. Its pleasant and refreshing spearmint flavor is often used to spice up salads and sauces. Mint leaves are also dried and used to prepare fresh herbal tea or domestic herbal medicines.

How to cultivate: Mint only requires fertile, moist soil and direct sunlight. It is very adaptable and can thrive in most situations; it is not prone to frost damage.

Coriander: This is also called Coriandrum sativum or Chinese parsley. It is a delicate and short-lived annual, which is only grown from seeds planted at intervals throughout the growing season. The whole plant can be eaten; it is very popular in culinary culture and is typically used in Asian dishes, including Chinese and Thai meals.

Its leaves and seeds have very distinct flavors. The seeds taste a little like lemons and can be crushed to be used as a spice. The leaves are more bitter and can be chopped up and used to garnish meals. Besides its many culinary uses, it has many health benefits as well and is a major ingredient in herbal remedies worldwide.

How to cultivate: Coriander enjoys fertile soil and adequate sunlight. It prefers partial shade as this prevents the seeds from setting prematurely.

Dill: This herb is also called Anethum graveolens, and it is a hardy but short-lived annual. It is relatively easy to grow from seed in your raised bed, and can be used for a variety of things like cooking and production of certain cosmetics. Dried or fresh dill leaves with their wonderful fragrance combine beautifully with seafood like smoked salmon. It is also popularly paired with soups and potatoes.

How to cultivate: Grow in moist soil where enough warmth can surround the herb. Partial shade is preferred to prevent the premature setting of the seed.

Fennel: This indigenous Mediterranean herb, also called Foeniculum vulgare, will make a lovely addition to your herb garden. Also native to the Mediterranean, it can be cultivated from seed in the UK. Despite being a hardy perennial, fennel is usually grown annually to maintain its crop. It is highly aromatic with an aniseed flavor, which makes it an amazing ingredient for both savory and sweet dishes. Its young, delicate leaves can be used as a garnish in soups, salads, and with seafood sauce, as well as in sticky, sweet, delicious puddings and sauces. The whole plant is edible, making it a versatile herb.

How to cultivate: This is an especially robust herb that grows well in any soil if it is placed under direct sunlight.

French Tarragon: The French tarragon is also called Artemisia dracunculus, and despite being a little tricky to cultivate, this herb is loved by culinary enthusiasts, particularly those of the French cuisine. It has a sweet anise aroma and licorice flavor. It is considered the finest of all tarragon varieties in the kitchen. It is especially delicious when combined with chicken, but it is also used to season oils, vinegar, and béarnaise sauce.

How to cultivate: Despite being perennial, it is prone to rotting out in over-saturated soils and wet regions, so take care to plant in partially dry soil and not water excessively. Cultivate in fertile soil where it can receive adequate amounts of sunlight and warmth to produce shoots in abundance.

The French tarragon rarely blossoms, so seed production is greatly limited. It cannot be cultivated from seed and must be grown through root division. Divide the roots in spring to maintain its health, and replant every two of three years.

Parsley: This popular herb is also called Petroselinum crispum, and is an absolute must in your herb garden. It is a hardy biennial grown from seed every year in summer and spring.

It is used to prepare Middle Eastern salads, pesto paired with basil, and used in fishcakes and stews. Curly parsley is very decorative due to its curly leaves and is used to garnish many dishes.

How to cultivate: For the most productive results, plant this in the fertile soil of your vegetable raised bed. Water regularly during prolonged periods of drought. Parsley tolerates a little shade, although it loves direct sunlight. There are two kinds of parsley cultivated in Europe: The flat-leaf and curly parsley. The flat-leaf is more popular because it is more tolerant of sunshine and rain, and has a stronger flavor, according to some.

Rosemary: This herb is also known as Rosemarinus officinalis, and it is considered great for brain health. It is believed by the Greeks to be linked to having a good memory and cognitive function. It is an especially nutritious herb to cultivate in your herb garden. Being an evergreen shrub, it is available all year round and has aromatic leaves that are beautifully shaped like needles to adorn your garden. Rosemary is also considered a decorative plant because of its white, purple, and pink flowers. Combine rosemary with roast meats such as chicken and lamb, and use it as a flavoring in Yorkshire puddings and stuffing.

How to cultivate: This herb thrives in well-drained soil, under direct sunlight. It is resistant to pests and tolerant to dry spells, but not for long periods.

Sage: Also called Salvia officinalis, this herb is known for its intense flavor and slightly peppery and savory taste, making it one of the most widely grown and used herbs in Britain. Its green and white and purple variegated forms make it an exceptional source of adornment for herb gardens, particularly because it can also act as an ornamental border. This kitchen essential is often used in stuffing and paired with pork.

The usual property of this herb is the significant increase in flavor as the leaves grow, so the bigger the leaves, the tastier the dish. Besides being a good source of Vitamin C, it is rich in other minerals like potassium.

How to cultivate: This evergreen shrub will be available to you year-round if it is cultivated in well-drained areas with lots of sunlight.

How to Dry Herbs

Airdrying

1. Select about five to ten branches and hold them together with a rubber band or string. The fewer the branches, the quicker they will dry.

2. Place the bundle of herbs in a paper bag with the stem side facing up. Use a string to seal the bag closed, ensuring that you don't crush any herbs. Now make a few holes in the bag for air circulation.

3. String the bag up by the stem end in a warm, well-ventilated area.

4. Your herbs should be dried and ready for storage in a week.

Oven-Drying

1. Spread the herbs on a cookie sheet with a depth of 1 inch or less.

2. Slide the sheet pan into an open oven and let it dry on low heat for two to four hours.

3. To test if the herbs are dry enough, touch the leaves to see if they crumble easily. Herbs dried in the oven tend to cook a bit during the process, which removes some of the flavor and potency, so you might need twice the normal amount when using them for cooking.

4. Preserve the herbs in airtight containers like plastic storage cabinets, freezer Ziplock bags, and canning jars. For the perfect flavor, don't crush the leaves until you are prepared to use them. Also, be sure to exhaust them in a year.

Freezing

Certain herbs retain their flavor best when frozen. They include dill, basil, lemon balm, chervil, mint, chives, rosemary, thyme, parsley, lemon verbena, French tarragon, sage, and oregano.

1. Wash the herbs properly and pat or shake to get rid of the excess water. You can chop them before storing them if you like.

2. Put the whole or chopped leaves in freezer bags and flatten them to get rid of air.

Rosemary, thyme, dill, and sage freeze well on their stalks, which can be added to cooking pots frozen and removed before serving. You can also blend the herbs into a puree with a little amount of water and freeze the paste in freezer bags. When you are ready to use them, simply chip off the frozen pieces and throw them into your pot.

Mix herbs that are good cooking companions such as thyme and sage. Throw them in a blender with a drizzle of olive oil and puree until smooth paste forms. Pour the mixture directly into freezer bags or ice cube trays and then freezer bags.

Chapter Ten: Growing Flowers in Raised Beds

The most vital reason to plant some flowers in your raised beds is to draw in native bees and other pollinators. If bees don't make a pit stop at your garden for a quick nectar snack and to throw some pollen around, you will be pretty disappointed with your crops. Besides, cultivating bee-friendly flowers in your garden supports biodiversity and struggling pollinator colonies. There are so many flowers particularly designed to attract hummingbirds, butterflies, and other nectar-loving species.

Before you make any seed purchases, here are a few important tips to remember when choosing flower varieties for your raised bed garden.

- Take note of bloom time: To succeed in companion planting with flowers, you need to choose flowers with the same bloom time as your vegetable crops. If the flowers you settle on do not bloom until three weeks after your peas are done flowering, your peas will not benefit from that companionship. Seed packets will give you the necessary information about the flower, including its bloom time, so you can synchronize your planting schedule. Grow a variety of flowers with different bloom times to ensure that all or most of your veggies benefit from the experience.

• Consider the flower shape: The flowers that draw in beneficial wasps or bees are not the same kind of flowers that pull in hummingbirds. The shape of the flower makes access to nectar and pollen harder or easier for different species. If you are looking to attract pollinators like bees, consider flowers with a composite shape like daisies, purple coneflowers, zinnias, sunflowers, and cosmos.

• Spread them out: Don't plant all your flowers in one section of the garden; space them out. How you do this is your decision, but there are many ways to go about it. You can cultivate a row of flowers right after a row of vegetables, or you can plant one flower between two vegetables. Come up with your own strategies, like using flowers as a border or to break up a row as an indicator of where a certain vegetable ends and others begin.

• Consider the height of the flower: You don't want flowers that will compete with your crops for sunlight so go for primarily low-growing flowers. For instance, certain crops like spinach might appreciate a little shade during the warmer months, so the height of your flowers depends on their location and the crops in your garden.

• Start with simple flowers: If you are a beginner, I recommend that you begin with annuals because they are easy to grow and produce a lot of blooms. Also, you won't need to worry about them sprouting in the same spot next year if you intend to change the design of your garden. One of the most effective ways to attract native bees is to plant native perennials, so plant them in small amounts; you know what will work best for your garden.

Quick Glossary

1. **Perennial:** Any plant that flowers year after year. The leaves typically fall to the ground in autumn, die, and then regrow the next season. Some perennials last longer than others like peony rose, while others don't last past a few years.

2. **Annual:** Any plant with a growth cycle of one year. Annuals are typically hardy crops and remain unaffected by frost. A great example is calendula.

3. **Half-Hardy Annual:** Any annual that is delicate. They are usually cultivated indoors or in warm areas like greenhouses, then cautiously exposed to cold conditions outdoors now and then before being transplanted outdoors after the threat of frost is over. For example, you have marigolds, cosmos, and so on.

4. **Biennial:** Any plant with a growth cycle of two years. Biennial seeds are usually sown around April of the first year. The leaves mature the same year and then flower the next year. Examples are wallflowers, foxgloves, and so on.

20 Best Flowers for Raised Beds

- **Himalayan Blue Poppy:** This is a perennial with gorgeous sky-blue color. It is a half-hardy crop that enjoys little moisture. Remove the flower buds in the first year to prevent them from blooming; otherwise, they may become reluctant to bloom again.

- **Annual Poppies:** These are relatively easy to plant from seed. They produce a lot of seeds in late summer and early fall. The seeds can be harvested and stored in a cool, dry place like a paper bag until next season when they can be scattered to sprout new plants.

- **Aubrieta:** This perennial is considered a ground covering plant, making it suitable for raised beds and walls. It can sometimes sprout from cracks in the wall and pavement, spreading several feet away from its origin. It can be found in pink, rose, lilac, and purple colors. This flower can last for as long as ten years or more.

- **Red Valerian:** This flower is available in white, red, and pink colors. It is commonly found growing in the wild, ruins, and on old walls and bridges. It can spread throughout your garden and become a weed if left out of control. It is a very hardy plant and can withstand extremely cold temperatures.

- **Delphinium:** These perennials are tall and have spikes. They have sky-blue, violet, and white variations. They can withstand low temperatures with no form of damage to their roots, but they must be staked to prevent them from being flattened or blown away by heavy winds. As perennials, they can last for as long as twenty years. They also produce seeds that can be stored and easily planted the next year.

- **Geraniums:** These are the same as pelargoniums, which are also called geraniums. These herbaceous perennials come in a variety of beautiful colors. They are capable of self-seeding and spreading all over your garden if not controlled.

- **Scabiosa:** This is a perennial that has cream, lavender-blue, and lilac varieties. They require little attention, but you must remove the dead heads for new buds to form. It has a relative tolerance of low temperatures.

- **Perennial Flax:** Also called blue flax, this plant has beautiful sky-blue flowers adorning slim, tender stems. Their flowers last only a day but are constantly replaced by new ones. It is one of the short-lived perennials.

- **Livingstone Daisies:** Also called mesembryanthemum, these flowers are the low-growing kind. They are also annuals and quite easy to plant from seed. When they bloom, the flowers are multi-petaled with a variety of colors. The petals open in the daytime and close at night.

- **Bellflower:** Also called Campanula, this ground-covering plant is a low-growing perennial with lilac flowers shaped like a small bell. It grows rapidly and spreads over rocks and walls.

- **Rockrose:** These are sub-shrubs that grow rapidly and are great for edging. They thrive in direct sunlight and well-drained soil.

- **Silver Ragwort:** This biennial is also called the dusty miller. It is a Mediterranean native popular for its ornamental silver-colored leaves. It is relatively hardy and can survive hot temperatures with little scorch damage. Being a biennial, the seeds are typically planted in April on trays and transplanted to raised beds or pots once they sprout their first pairs of true leaves. Like all biennials, it blooms in the summer of the next year. It is also toxic and must be kept out of reach of livestock and children.

- **Foxgloves:** These are biennials just like silver ragwort, so the planting process is the same. Sow the seeds in April, transplant in the fall, and then watch them bloom in the summer of next year. Environmental regulations in some regions ban digging up of plants from the wild and replanting in your garden. However, this biennial is quite easy to grow from seed. They are relatively tall plants with spikes and purple flowers shaped like bells.

- **Oriental Poppies:** These are relatively easy to grow from seed. They are typically sown in spring and germinated near a hot water tank or in a warm room of 17°C. Spread the seed on a tray layered with compost and sprinkle some extra compost on the top to sow. They must be transplanted into raised beds or pots once they are sufficiently large.

- **Feverfew:** This perennial herb is adorned with white daisy-like blooms. It self-seeds readily and will spread to all parts of your garden if you don't keep it under control. Some people are not very fond of white flowers, but a splash of white here and there can balance out the striking colors in your garden. This plant is popular for its fast action on migraines if the leaves are infused into hot water to make an herbal tea or chewed raw, although I don't recommend that because it is BITTER.

- **Oregano:** This perennial herb is known for its subtle but beautiful flowers. Its stems are adorned with little pale pink flowers when it blooms throughout summer. It is a hardy shrub capable of colonizing your garden if you let it. It is also a favorite of bees, butterflies, and chefs!

- **Pot Marigolds:** These are also called calendulas. They are hardy annuals quite easy to grow from seeds. They readily self-seed and are available in yellow and orange varieties.

- **Hyacinths:** Flowers usually have no other choice but to brighten up the garden in spring, but hyacinths arrive late to the party with their splashes of color in late spring and early summer. They are grown from bulbs and are typically sown in autumn to bloom in March and April. They are naturally hardy but can be conditioned to be delicate if cultivated in pots. When shopping for hyacinth bulbs, buy the ones with a 'prepared' label on them. This variety needs to be forced and should be sown in late September in a cool place with a temperature of about 50 degrees Fahrenheit for about eight to ten weeks. Then they are ready to be placed in indoor raised beds to flower in approximately three weeks. Hyacinths come in varieties of white, purple, and various shades of blue.

- **Red Campion:** This perennial is a wild one and breathtakingly beautiful. It is available in varieties of pink and red and, like many wildflowers, red campion isn't as flamboyant as the flashy bedding plants popularly used in planters. When paired with other wild plants to form a border, the result is more natural and subtle. The individual seeds are generally available for purchase, but if not, ask your seed provider if they can be added to a packet of different wildflower seeds.

Chapter Eleven: Preparing Your Beds for Next Year

Fall is finally here and, as expected, it brings with it the inevitable slowing of activity in every garden. Based on your location, perennials may have started blushing with beautiful colors and shedding their leaves.

Annual veggies are reaching the end of their lifespan and are beginning to yield to the nip of progressively heavier frosts. Following the rush of spring sowing and the peak of summer's reaping, it is tempting to pull the curtain, sit back, and just let nature do its thing. You already did the heavy lifting in spring and reaped the benefits in summer. What else is there to do now that fall is here?

The answer to that question depends on how smoothly you'd like to transition into spring when it rolls around. A few cautious steps executed this season will save you a lot of time and effort in the long haul. If you'd rather lessen the work that comes with the start of next year's growing season, then take some of these suggestions into consideration. Let's look at the steps to put your garden to bed:

1. Gather up and dispose of finished and rotting plants: besides the unattractive look they add to your garden, old plants can harbor fungi, diseases, and pests. As noted by the Cooperative Extension of

Colorado State University, unwanted pests and insects who feed on your plants throughout summer may deposit eggs on their leaves and stalks. Getting rid of spent plants from the surface of the soil keeps pests from getting a head start when spring rolls around. You can also bury them in garden trenches if they are free of diseases, as this improves soil health by contributing organic matter to the soil.

2. Get rid of invasive weeds that may have spread over the growing season: Remember the intruding Himalayan blackberry? Or the bindweed that took over your raspberry patch? The time to get rid of those renegades is now. Pull them out of the soil with their roots and trash or burn them. A lot of invasive weeds remain active in weed piles or compost heaps, so don't give in to the urge to move them to another section of your garden. Getting rid of invasive plants is the only way to keep them from growing all over again and being their disruptive selves when spring comes back.

3. Your soil needs to be prepared for spring: Even though many gardeners would rather perform this activity when spring comes around, fall is a good time for soil preparation like adding manure, bone meal, rock phosphate, compost, and kelp. In most regions, the climate allows these new additions to break down, enrich your soil, and become biologically active. It also means there will be no need to wait until your garden is dry enough in spring to be worked on for the first time.

Turning, digging, and amending your soil now gives you some time off when the season hits because you will have already done most of the work. Also, tilling in fall helps boost soil drainage before intense weather becomes a reality. Once you have made all the necessary amendments according to your soil needs in fall, layer the bed with sheet plastic or any other safe covering to keep winter rains from sinking the newly added nutrients below the active root zone. This applies to all types of gardens but especially to raised beds because they drain more effectively than ground beds. Take the sheeting off in early spring and use a hoe to till lightly before planting.

4. Consider planting cover crops: In many climates, early fall or late summer is a great time to plant cover crops like clover, rye, or vetch. These crops help protect your soil from erosion, boost levels of organic matter, and break up firmly packed areas. Cover crops also contribute to the nutrient content of the soil. Planting legumes like field peas or clover in your raised beds helps to enhance your soil's nitrogen levels, which is an important aspect of vegetable gardening. It is recommended to plant cover crops about a month or more before the first killing frost hits, but certain cover crops are stronger than others, so check with your seed provider or local extension officer to know the best cover crops for your region.

5. Prune your perennials: Fall is a great time to prune perennial garden crops, although you should be cautious when choosing the ones to prune. For instance, fennel likes to be pruned in the fall. Research has shown that dead raspberry canes continue to feed the plant's crown well into the winter. Blueberries also like to be pruned in spring as it helps protect them from stress and disease. Direct your fall pruning efforts to herbs like thyme, sage, and rosemary, and vegetables like rhubarb and asparagus. Blackberries also like to be cleaned up nicely in the fall. Get rid of any crossing or spent canes to help control the plant's aggressive spread.

6. Consider dividing and planting bulbs: Despite the flowering and death of spring bulbs, other flowering bulbs like lilies bloom in fall. Wait until three or four weeks after the bloom to dig up and divide any crowded or straggly plants during this season. Lift the bulbs carefully and divide bulblets to be transplanted immediately to another section of the garden. If you dug up your spring bulbs before fall rolled around, now is a great time to replant them. Crocuses, daffodils, and tulips should be ready to get back into the soil for another glorious display next season.

7. Harvest your compost pile: Now that the summer heat is done and the microbes of nature are getting ready for their winter nap, it is tempting to ignore the compost pile, but I'll tell you the two ways this

can be a missed opportunity. First, materials left to decompose over the summer are done and ready for use. This rich material should be layered on garden beds to fix deficient soil, fertilize lawns if any, or generally top up the garden bed. This will nourish your plants and give their growth a jump start when spring comes around. Second, clearing out your compost heap will make way for a fresh batch, which can be insulated against frost, meaning that microbes can get to work even in the winter. Pile up lots of autumn leaves, sawdust, or straw, and layer them with scraps from the kitchen and any other active green matter you can lay your hands on, to keep those microbes working for longer on your fresh compost pile.

8. Replenish the mulch: Mulching in winter has a lot of similar benefits with mulching in summer. They include a significant reduction in water loss, protection from erosion, and prevention of weeds. Mulching in the winter has more benefits because as the soil transitions to colder temperatures, the freezing and melting of the soil can have adverse effects on the crops whose roots have to go through all the churning and heaving associated with the transition. Layering the soil with a mulch helps with temperature and moisture regulation, which eases these effects. Piling a thick layer of mulch around the root crops left in your raised beds this season can act as a buffer against killer frosts and prolong the life of your crops. Plus, the mulch decomposes to add fresh organic material to your soil.

9. Assess your growing season and review the cultivars: Did your selection of fruits and vegetables perform as well as you hoped this season? The time to reconsider under-performing crops is now. You need to take stock and discover if there are plants to be replaced, and if better varieties are available for your location. If your crops did as well as you hoped, I suggest extending the harvest by adding varieties that ripen later or earlier in the season. When taking stock of vegetable performance, take cautious notes about what worked and what didn't to prepare for next season. Some failures and successes of the season can be because of the climate, but other factors can be

controlled like moisture levels, plant orientation, and soil fertility. Keep a record of the lessons you learned this season, the highs and the lows of summer, as they will act as a reference for the next planting season.

10. Care for your tools: Taking care of your tools is a given in gardening, and most gardeners know this. This crucial task can seem overwhelming when the farming season is back, and there is just so much to do. Fall is the perfect time to show your tools some love and affection. Start by washing them to get rid of dirt and debris. If a tool is rusty, file it with a wire brush or sandpaper. Use a basic mill file to sharpen shovels and hoes. Use a whetstone to sharpen pruning shears and other bladed tools. Finally, clean all the tools with a rag lightly coated in machine oil. This helps protect the metal from oxygen and extend the lifespan of your tools for the next season.

The Importance of Foresight

Regardless of where you live, there will always be steps to take to prepare for the next gardening season, as outlined above. When you take these steps, they will not only ensure a smooth transition into the next farming season; they will also boost your harvests in the long-term.

Preparing for a New Raised Bed

If you plan on purchasing new raised beds next season, the best thing to do is get them ready the fall before. As we discover more information about soil health, especially the economically important microbes that live in the soil, we realize the importance of having a head start on certain processes before the plants are ready to be cultivated. This way, they get settled in and established more quickly than usual, and remain healthy for as long as those conditions are maintained. Amending and tilling the soil long before any planting allows the soil to come alive over the winter season. Some gardeners like to call this process "building a living soil profile," and it needs some time to activate. This process can be done with ease and involve a few simple steps.

First, select a location for your new bed and mark it off with a barrier. Once that is done, use a shovel or tiller to turn the soil over. Now pour in your compost. If you have domestic animals, their poop can serve as composted manure, but any good compost will suffice. Some people make theirs; others make purchases. If you want to go down that path, as long as it isn't sterilized, you're good to go.

Another great source of compost is the pile of leaves being shed this time of year. If you have a mower fitted with a bag, shred the leaves before using them. If not, just pour them directly on the bed whether they are fresh or not, because they will be decomposed by the time its farming season. Those important microbes we talked about will get to work on them.

Don't manage your compost. Pile it up as high as 4 to 6 inches, especially if it's free. Begin by layering the surface of the soil and then work it into the soil with either a tiller or shovel. When that is all done, get a hand rake and level your garden bed.

The next thing to do is absolutely nothing. Just sit back and let nature take the wheel. What will happen next is those important microbes will come alive and grow inside your soil. To give the process a jumpstart and take things up a few notches, you can throw in a microbial drench. These are packed with a crazy amount of microbes, and all you must do is water them into your composted soil. They will begin to eat the compost, breaking it down in the process and turning it into nutrients that will be eaten by your plants when the spring rolls around.

The other amazing part about setting up a bed now is that garden chores are usually at a minimum during the fall. This gives you ample time to do it right without having to worry about watering, fertilizing, or weeding other raised beds. The key to a healthy and productive garden is a solid foundation, and that foundation is your garden bed.

Take the right preparatory steps, and your gardening will be a lot easier and more productive.

Chapter Twelve: The Importance of Charting Your Progress

Keeping a record of your progress and the happenings in your garden is something most gardeners start enthusiastically but eventually let fall by the wayside. When the crops start growing and you begin to reap the harvests, it is easy to forget to take notes. The usefulness of the information and photos taken during the growing season is so underrated. With a journal, you can look at things in retrospect, seeing the problems you had and the time they occurred, the plants that flourished, and the ones that didn't.

Here, I will outline an easy method for keeping track of the things you planted and where you planted them. All your questions might not necessarily be answered, but it will give you a head start. Let's start with the supplies you will need to begin your garden journal:

1. Three-Ring Binder: Any binder will suffice, but if you intend to take your journal into your garden now and then, a vinyl binder is a perfect option. Get a binder that zips shut, making it easy to slip things into it even when you're in a hurry and not having to worry about them slipping out. You can also get one with a cover that lets you slide a photo of your favorite container, plant, or raised bed.

2. Plastic Photo Sleeves: Plastic sheets are relatively cheap and are sold at craft stores at a discount. Sleeves the size of baseball cards are also available and sold in bulk, but they are too small for some seed packets, so get them in a variety of sizes for seed packets, photos, and tags.

3. Blank Pages: Put blank pages in the back of your journal for extra notes. If you make notes somewhere else for some reason, you can always slide them into a sleeve.

4. Permanent Markers: You will need at least one of these for longer notes.

5. Seed Packets and Plant Tags: Store them as you plant.

6. Calendar: This will enable you to keep track of your planting days and any other event significant to your garden.

7. Pictures of your Garden: Ensure you take photos of the good and bad. Most of the time, we don't think to take pictures of insect damage and diseases, but they are just as important as the blooming flowers.

Starting Your Garden Journal

Once you have gathered all your journal supplies, now you must tuck things into your plastic sleeves. Preserve all your seed packets and plant tags by slipping them into the sleeve pockets. For convenience, keep information about each raised bed or garden section in a separate sleeve to make it easier to find information about your plants based on their location.

Now that you have all that information in one place, the next course of action is note-taking. The packets and tags give you information on your plants instantly. Both sides of a sleeve are see-through, so you'll be able to easily obtain plant identification and the notes on their development.

Your permanent markers will help you make more notes. You can start by marking the raised bed or area of the garden directly on the plastic sleeve with distinct colors. You can also take notes of all the details like when a plant first bloomed, the harvest you obtained, the day you planted a crop, and where it was purchased.

All you need to get started on this is a fine tip marker. You can get more creative with stickers, glitter, markers, and other items from the craft store if you wish. If you have a calendar, it will serve as a handy reference for all the significant dates like the day crops were planted, pruned, and harvested, even when they bloomed or wilted.

Taking Photos for Your Journal

Taking photos for documentation is not only an amazing way to keep track of your garden's progress, but it also acts as a trigger for your memory years or even months after you began keeping records.

As your garden progresses and your plants are sprouting, take and print shots of your favorite scenes and great combinations. Shoot the same spot at different times, on different days, to observe the progression. Take photos of the raised beds or containers you would like to duplicate. Try using the black and white picture trick where you observe photos without the distraction of color. Pictures are also a nice way to take notes about crops that need to be moved or divided and colors that are striking or are too dull.

Also, make sure that you take shots of diseased crops and pest infestations to keep track of the issue. Endeavor also to take pictures of any area with issues, no matter what they are, to study them and correct the problem during the off-season. Don't worry; no one else has to see them but you.

Making Use of Your Garden Journal

Now that you have all the necessary tips, it is time to put them to work. Typically, you will have to take your journal with you into the garden to take quick notes, but having all the pictures, plant tags, and seed packets will enable you to go through your garden from the comfort of your study or bedroom and jot down all the important notes and reminders

Specific Tracking Suggestions

1. The crop you planted and where you planted it.

2. When you began seeds.

3. Sections of the garden that need to be worked on.

4. Issues to closely observe.

5. Crops that need to be moved or divided.

6. Overgrown areas of your garden.

7. Crops that require attention in spring.

8. Where crops were planted in preparation for crop rotation and much more.

As time passes, you will discover many other uses for your garden journal, and you will be grateful for keeping one when the time comes to purchase more seeds or plants in preparation for the next season. And if you ever relocate, it will be easy for you to compile a plant list with the necessary information for the next owner of the property- assuming your raised bed is fixed, and the new owners are into gardening.

If you keep an ornamental garden, making notes is equally useful, especially as you try out new plants every season. If you'd rather tend to the same plants every season, I suggest a perpetual journal. It is similar to the normal journal because you will still store plant tags and seed packets in sleeves, but you can also keep a running record of your garden's progress every year. Do this and watch your journal evolve to suit your gardening style.

Conclusion

Raised beds have been around longer than the word itself. Since they are simply gardens where the soil is elevated from the ground, other advantages besides aesthetics might not be obvious to many people, well, except people with bad backs who see the convenience at first glance.

You don't need a raised bed to cultivate great-tasting fruits, vegetables, and herbs because almost any ground bed with maximum sunlight can do that. However, raised bed gardening stands out because of its numerous advantages you are now aware of. For one thing, it is incomparably easier on the back, as it involves less bending over.

Raised beds are your opportunity to start over with uncontaminated and enriched soil. Suppose you lived on sloped property; no worries because raised beds offer level and convenient planting areas. Plus, they warm up faster than ground beds in the spring, so you get a head start when it's growing season.

The numerous advantages will not do much for you if you neglect your soil, and that is one of the most common mistakes made by beginning gardeners. When your soil is healthy and packed with nutrients and organic matter, your crops will be more robust and practically care for themselves. With raised beds, you get to water and weed less and worry less about pests and insect attacks. With raised beds, you call the shots.

This book has provided practical advice on the kind of mulches and frame materials to use, different ways to boost soil fertility, seed selection, and lots of options to choose from including the different options for irrigation, pest prevention tactics, and much more. You have all you need to know to get started on raised bed gardening. It is the perfect blend of convenience and productivity, and I know that you will have as much fun gardening as you hoped!

Here's another book by Dion Rosser that you might like

Printed in Great Britain
by Amazon